# The Year

A Crack the Spine Literary Anthology

Executive Editor: Kerri Farrell Foley

Published by Crack the Spine
Executive Editor: Kerri Farrell Foley
Co-Editors: Laura Huey Chamberlain, Jacob
Guajardo, Preston Taylor Stone, Suke Cody,
Olivia Kiers, Naomi Danae, Elizabeth
McIntosh, Courtney LeBlanc, Konstantin Rega,
Becca Wild, Michelle Donfrio
Crack the Spine is a production of
Quartermarch Media, LLC
ISBN-13: 978-1-7328693-4-9
ISSN: 2474-9095

# CONTENTS

# LETTER FROM THE EDITOR

This anthology seeks to provide a service. Our world moves at an increasingly rapid pace; words and memories become disposable, and we often find ourselves stopping to ask, "how did we get here?" This book serves as a record of our world as it changed.

Much has been said about 2020. It was easily the most traumatic year in my life, personally, and I know that the work of creatives around the world reflected this trend as well. Now that some distance has been achieved, perhaps we are able to look at the disjointed and unprecedented evens of the previous years with something resembling a reflective acceptance.

I ask the reader to be prepared for stories dealing with sexual assault, gun violence, and other challenging topics. We publish these works not to trigger or to shock our audience, but because they are intrinsically tied to the conversations and events we experienced in 2020, both as individuals, and as a collective society.

Kerri Farrell Foley

# WHERE DO YOU GET YOUR IDEAS?

## LINDA TRICE

Maybe this wasn't such a good idea after all, Lisa thought as she gazed out a bedroom window. There was green as far as she could see. Green grass, green trees, green grassy hills and not a single building anywhere.

She'd moved into the house yesterday. It was just what she'd told the real estate person she needed. Lisa's Greenwich Village apartment in Manhattan was so noisy that she wasn't able to write. She was sure that an award winning book was in her if only she had the right environment. Oh, for serenity. Oh, for the quiet country life. Oh, for inspiration.

So here she was in the midst of serenity and quiet. Where was the inspiration?

She heard a knock at the front door.

Lisa ran to the door then stopped. As a native New Yorker she knew better than to throw the door open. Who knew what evil lurked on the other side?

Wait, Lisa thought. I'm not in the city. There are no

muggers or serial killers out here in the country.

Maybe it was a woodpecker? How did they sound? She had no idea.

The knock came again.

Lisa looked out the living room window.

A large woman wearing a dowdy blue flowered house dress stood on the porch. Who was she?

"Hello! I know you're in there," the woman called out in an overbearing voice. Then she knocked louder. She was persistent.

Lisa cautiously opened the door. A large, strongly built woman with a wicker basket on her arm pushed the door open and strode in. "I'm Mrs. Mason, Mary Mason," she told Lisa. She brushed past the younger woman, marched through the living room and straight into the kitchen.

Lisa closed the front door, turned the two locks and fastened the security chain she'd brought from Manhattan. When she got in her kitchen the woman was filling an old fashioned tea kettle. "When people move in, they often can't find exactly what they're looking for," Mrs. Mason explained. Then Mrs. Mason pulled out cups, saucers, a tin of loose tea and warm apple muffins from the wicker basket.

There was another knock at the door.

"Do get that dear," Mrs. Mason said. "That will be Gertrude."

Lisa admitted Gertrude who was bent over from the huge, plastic box she carried in both arms. She placed it on Lisa's table with a thud then removed a baked ham and casserole sized bowls of potato salad.

There was another knock and Petunia Peabody entered with pink lemonade and strawberry cupcakes.

The yard rapidly filled with people, cars, trucks, a few saddle horses and a retired school bus. Children screeched as they happily chased each other across the grass. Teens set up a stage for dancing and hooked up a generator powered sound system.

Men unfolded long metal tables on the lawn and carried china plates from the back of cars. Bo Wilson fired up his gas powered grill. "He'll take any opportunity to use it," Mrs. Mason told Lisa. "Now dear, you'd better go and put your costume on."

Costume?

The women in the kitchen stopped what they were doing and stared at Lisa.

"You must be in costume before the sun sets or you'll be turned to stone," Mrs. Mason said.

Lisa stared at her, stunned.

"The real estate agent should have given you one," Petunia Peabody softly said.

Lisa blinked then leaned against the kitchen counter. She blinked again. She looked at the people crowded in her kitchen. They were serious. This was not some kind of joke. They really believed this costume story.

"The house is haunted," Mrs. Mason explained.

The sun began to sink.

Gertrude gave Lisa a cup of strong tea with a lot of

sugar in it. Bo poured in a jigger of rum. "Forget her costume?" he asked Mrs. Mason.

Outside, the teen band played, girls sang, an MC announced a fashion show and little kids screamed happily as they continued to chase each other.

Mrs. Mason escorted Lisa across the grassy green lawn towards a stone fence.

Lisa sat on the stones, still bewildered by the events that had taken place within the last few hours.

Bo handed Lisa a plate piled high with his award winning barbeque and Millie Gribbles' baked beans. Lisa snatched one of Petunia Peabody's strawberry cupcakes and greedily gobbled it. Then she looked down and noticed that all the stones on the fence had wrinkles, like withered faces.

She couldn't feel her feet.

The tips of her fingers tingled.

Her eyes closed, and the china tea cup fell from her hand.

"It's happening." Mrs. Mason was excited. "Go get my daughter," she ordered Gertrude. "She needs to see this. She's always complaining that she has nothing to write about."

# CORNFIELD CONSTELLATIONS

## LIZA SOFIA

I roll down my window on the carriageway to get a better look at the sky. It's a good thing I'm not driving because I can't keep my eyes from drifting up to those ethereal clouds above us. I point out a pair of dancing squirrels in the sky, with their bushy tails intertwined, and tell you it reminds me of when I used to live in Boston and feed squirrels at the Common in the evenings. And just ahead of us is an antique butter churn that I tell you reminds me of my first-grade field trip to an 18th-century manor. You can't see either. But that's alright. I'm happy to explain each cloud as we drive by. Though, I don't think that the miles and miles of cornfields stretched out ahead of us is enough.

I'm getting scared the road will run out.

I ask you to pull over every time we pass a patch of land with grass cut low enough for us to lay on, but you say we can't because it's private property. There isn't a foot of terrain that isn't private property. There's always some pesky red barn attached to it like a tick you can't shake off.

Though, I can't blame them for wanting to own the land and the clouds above it. Everyone likes watching clouds—the same way everyone likes watching sunsets and meteor showers and shooting stars. Because it makes you feel small in the grand scheme of the universe. But not right now. Right now, I'm an ancient Greek god riding through crop fields in a light blue Hyundai Sonata chariot, telling you the myths behind each of my constellations.

It's getting darker now.

You know I've never liked the heat, but for once, I want the sun to stay in the sky just a little longer.

I think about taking your hand off the steering wheel and trace the outline of the long vined potted plant that almost fell on my head as a toddler, but I doubt you'd see it anyways. Instead, I take your hand and hold it tight in mine and silently vow to tell you these stories tomorrow.

# BLACK WAVES CRASHING ON A BLUE SHORE

## TAIN LEONARD-PECK

Voices cry, loud, true,

at the line, black, blue; kneel if

not the enemy.

# THIS MORNING AFTER THE RIOTS

## AE HINES

Like the weather of my childhood in the deep south.
Thunder crashing over our roof, rattling every window,

lightning, then hail firing down like bullets, pinging up
from the ground and ricocheting off the glass.

Last night, people who for weeks wore masks, marched
to downtown Portland and set fire to the courthouse.

They burned cars and broke windows. They hurled rocks
and firecrackers at police, then looted the Louis Vuitton.

All night, flash bangs, tear gas, the roar of helicopters.
This morning thunder and hail and rain.

In the South, sudden storms remained mysterious. Biblical.
Thunder, my grandmother explained, God moving his
furniture.

Rain, the angels crying over some injustice done to man
by other men. The sun still shining, the Devil, beating his
wife.

Another Memorial Day. Another bright Monday. The sun
glowering down, another white officer snuffing out

another innocent black life. This is not mysterious.
This is plain as the dead man's face.

"Be quiet," Grandma would say at any coming storm.
"The Lord is doing His work." And then it would thunder.

Then it would rain. We sat at her window, still as corpses,
and watched His bright finger crawl the dark, trembling
sky.

# MCDONALD'S

## DEVIN PORTER

### Kim

Four seventy-three. Four seventy-four. Four seventy-five.

I was heading home. (Beat.) 187 St. Francis Avenue. That's where I stayed. Been living in the same house since I was a little tyke. I was about 4 years old. Growing up, my father built the "Mathis Residence" from the ground up. Brick by Brick. Layer by Layer. And MY Blood, Sweat. Tears. Child Labor. Daddy had grab me each and every little red brick before he laid it down in the cement. I still have the cuts and scrapes on my hands from the sharp ones. But I ain't mad because it came out more beautiful than our church gatherings on Christmas Eve. The only time I ever leave that home is when I'm heading to work.

Four seventy-six. Four seventy-seven. Four seventy-eight.

I worked the graveyard shift at Mac-Donald's. Spent 12 years being the grill grandmaster. Flippin' dem chickens. Slammin' and Jammin'. Makin' them magnificent midnight burgers. You know it's real good when you tuck the pickles underneath the cheese. Just like you tucking your child in for a bedtime story. Then, you gotta put a lil' smiley face for the ketchup lines. Forget Chef Ramsey. Call me Chef Kimmie. Shitttttt. I ain't got my Employee of the Month picture up on that wall for no reason.

Four seventy-nine. Four eighty. Four eighty-one.

I was always ready go to war with that grill. From night till dawn, I was kickin' ass and takin' names. My battle scars ain't lie. I used to get these bumpy heat rashes, these juicy pimples, and these big ass boils too from the heat in the back. Some of them would come up oozing out on my forehead ready to explode like World War I. Boss lady Cheryl, always had me cleaning out the grease pit, wiping the adolescent piss off the toilet seats, and getting rid all that nasty hair in the bathroom sink. And if a customer got ever loud with me, whew child. I'm no boo boo the fool. "You ain't put no pickles on my burger, lady!" The pickles is underneath the cheese, baby. I wouldn't trade it for a thang in the world. After I would leave Mac-Donald's, I'd take the same path home. The same roads. The same 527 steps. Everyday. History repeats itself.

Four eighty-two. Four eighty-three. Four eighty—

There's an oak tree to my left with the initials carved T.M on it. There's an abandoned black Honda Civic on the right side of Jefferson. Another block down on Carter Street, I'd run into Miss April's dog, Christine the Chihuahua. I couldn't stand that little mole rat, but I love me some Miss April. On Sundays, she always stopped by my place and she'd make me these fantastic crispy double chocolate chunk cookies. Listen, I don't know what she did, but that white lady know how to make some chocolate chip cookies. I walked this path so much I could've of done this walk with my eyes closed. (Beat.) It was Friday night. The moon was shining bright. Not a problem in my sight, and I was just walkin'.

Four eighty-four. Four eighty-five. Four eighty—"You know it's late out here ma'am. Where you coming from?" I was a respectful cause I had somewhere to be. "Yeah, I know sir. Just walkin' back home from my job. Just tryna keep it moving along."

Four eighty-six. Four eighty-seven. Four— "Well, I ain't ever seen you in this neighborhood before."

Four eighty-eight. Four eighty-nine. Four eighty— "Did you hear me ma'am?" I smiled bigger than a slave answering her massa. "Yes, I did sir. I'm just heading home. That's-" "MA'AM. I need to see your ID."

So, I went into in my little knapsnack to grab my wallet and in the bat of an eye. I'm spread eagle. "My hands are up! They're up! Don't shoot! Please, don't shoot me officer!" 38 steps. My house was 38 steps away and— pop goes the weasel. (Beat.) I went blind that night. Once a year, I'd just walk this path to try to re-live the good ol' days. I just came from smelling them MacDonald's burgers. I couldn't get by the grill. So, I stood just outside and just——

(Kim inhales a deep breath.)

The burgers didn't smell the same. It's time for me to get to steppin'. It's not safe out here for people like me. History repeats itself.

(Beat)

Four ninety. Four ninety-one. Four ninety-two. Four ninety-three.

# HANDS NO HANDS

## BILL PRUITT

Hydrangeas at both sides of the house just losing their
color

Yellow maples in the dawn just getting theirs

A Kurdish defender of woman's rights has been murdered

because our president sent away the soldiers who
protected her


The moon of falling leaves has sunk behind the Green
Mountains to

the west, where the tall old Saguaro— also no longer
protected—

gives up its life for the border wall. It's every man for
himself, as if

survival was all that mattered, as if this place of autumn
splendor

where I have come to be with my grandchildren were not a
landscape of death

                    the moment I look at Twitter.

My granddaughter, ten, whisks eggs in a glass bowl.

Around her are hydrangeas and maples, and further

are the Kurds and their defenders

and the moon, missing an old friend in the desert.


Those who see it all and welcome and create,

You, reader, join hands with us.

Hands no hands.

Our circle is large

# COUNTRY POEM

## SARAH CAVAR

I might be made of ugly
houses sat ecstatic

row by row with            "us"
flags like clinging bluish scabs
to dying window-boxes.


I might be made of fingers

play Joan Baez's guitar
all sorrow-style - the color
of badmouthed bravado
blue
cover dixie like an old
plague blanket.


But still, the world
burns
calories            spinning

spite into a project

&nihilism into soap&

scab into a redblue bruise

&filth into a sick            beershaped

   fragrance

# SOUND BITES 2020

## WILLIAM R. STODDART

I sat in my easy chair and picked up the remote. It was the second week of the Senate hearings and they were scheduled to wrap things up today. I took aim at the television mounted on my living room wall then lowered my arm. Maybe I could start feeling better about things. I looked up at my half-painted ceiling, the other half waiting nineteen years for the absence of an excuse. I raised my arm. Aimed. Fired.

> *Protest was impotent. Opposition had been ruinous. It was time to have done with it and to start building up. The system which previously existed, and which was called democratic, had brought America to the verge of ruin. Democracy had brought ruin by mismanagement - only an organization made up of a strong, clearly defined leadership hierarchy could restore order again.*

*I, being an ardent patriot, allied myself with the man about whom I felt perceived most clearly the consequences of the Movement, and that probably he was the man who would find the ways and means to make America great again, to drain the proverbial swamp of leeches and mosquitoes living off the lifeblood of our Republic.*

*I did not want a war, nor did I bring it about. I did everything to prevent it by negotiations. After it had broken out, I did everything to assure victory. The only motive that guided me was my ardent love for my people, its happiness, its freedom, and its life. For this I call on my American patriots and the Almighty as witnesses.*

No more excuses. I opened the old paint and peeled moldy skin from the round jail of the can. I wiped dust from the label and read the sticker: **Color:** *Whitewash,* **Date:** *Sept. 2001.*

# EVERY CREATURE I WANNA KNOW

## BLAKE KILGORE

Bothersome leggy shoots climb out

and injure friends, mine and yours, not theirs. They have no friends.


We should poison them,

burn them out or drown them, pull them apart, remove them, and place them in the trash.


They are ugly, thorny, greedy and strong.

Robbers really, they take from our precious ones; sometimes they rape and kill.


It is true they can flourish in a desert of concrete.

Their wild nature lets them break rules, find crumbs the others ignore.

If you leave civilization, I mean, go way out,

you can see whole colonies of those unwanted - tall,
blooming red and yellow, black and white.


Lovely almost, if you let yourself forget what they are.

Let them have their space out there, away from us, among
their own, as it should be.


There's rumor some of them have powers,

something inside can heal the sick or comfort the weak
and sad.


Maybe that's true, but I don't know.

I'd rather not even think of them, so I kill them when I
can, in word or deed.


I have a neighbor; he doesn't see things like we do,

lets them in all the time, says it's natural, entices all kinds
of new and wondrous creatures.


I'll take my boxed hedgerow, my perfect edges and solitary
green.

Every creature I wanna know, I already met.

# SYMPTOMS OF WOKE-NESS IN THE WHITE MALE

## DAVID E. POSTON

Warning: may seem disoriented, downcast, or defensive

misses some dreams, mostly ones he was taught
in picture books as a child

> singing
>> *red & yellow, black & white*
>>> *they are precious in his sight*

never cared for Skittles—looks at hoodies
in     a     whole     different     way

voices in his head:
> Debbie Irving
>> Sherman Alexie
>>> Jimmy Santiago Baca

Claudia Rankine
            Tommy Orange
                        Ta-Nehisi Coates
Reginald Dwayne Betts
            Michelle Alexander
Isabel Wilkerson
            Robert F. Williams
James Baldwin
            Paul Mooney

friends whose jokes made him just a bit uncomfortable
now make him ashamed            of himself

Warning: may ask acquaintances of color
to pose with him for selfies

wonders why they call it a dog whistle
when everyone hears it

Warning: blurts out the story of his uncle,
family genealogist, sharing copies
of a will from the distaff side
bequeathing *one bed, one mule, & one negro boy*

can now talk about redlining, reparations, the historical inequities
of Social Security & the G.I. bill, mass incarceration,

the militarization of police departments,

or even how spell-check is a form of racist
microaggression,

but not about the girl of color

with whom he held hands at summer camp

when they were 16


understands the worst role to play now

is

    bystander

# A SPECTRUM OF DISORDER

## DENIEL SEAN MACAPAL

Flecks of color flew above me - blues and bright oranges. Hold my fingers out, the voices said. I squinted at the colors but I must have been misunderstood. They rushed at me, invading my air. Their queen, offended, smothered me with her royal robes. It didn't matter that I tried to scream - the voices merely expressed their delight. I only feared the queen who, with a single command, could tell her soldiers to nest in the hollow of my chest.

# MONTESQUIEU AND MULLEY'S CIRCUS FOR RESTLESS CHILDREN

## LIZA SOFIA

There is little I fear more than the October storms besides for dark-scaled serpents. Though, on this very night, I think I'd rather face the latter. I lie awake as the storm rages on just outside the thin walls of my bedroom. I hear the bustling of foliage, and imagine the wind striking the leaves of the tree by my window like a coiled viper. I slip deeper into my bed, pull the blanket higher up my neck- as though this barrier would protect me from the wraths of nature- or at the very least soothe me. It does very little to settle my jolting pulse. My only consolation are the shadows that flicker by the light of a small candle on the white wall opposite my bed- like little circus animals. The most dreadful part of the affair is the series of strikes- one monstrous roar after another. I haven't even the time to release my held breath. I am in the heart of one now- which each rumble more deafening than the last. I pull the covers over my head and shut my eyes until it has ended. I warily pull the blanket back.

There is a gust of warmed air against the small bit of my exposed cheek. I tilt my head the very slightest to see a pair of eyes. Golden eyes with dark dilated pupils. Ghostly wisps of breath escape from a black nose. A lion peeks his head through the 3 inch crack in the window which refuses to shut. I observe at the beast in disbelief. The lion bows his great maned head. Curious. I brush my trembling hand against its muzzle. The creature slips the rest of its body through the window as if there were no bones in its body. He sits at the foot of my bed and watches me, expectedly. I press the back of my hand against my forehead, but I do not feel feverish.

I suspend my belief in reality as they trickle in, one by one. A bear wearing a small star-patterned hat slips through the window, then a white stallion, two women dressed in cheetah leotards and an older gentleman with a long mustache. The candle goes out, leaving behind a light trail of grey smoke which rises to the ceiling and forms the words "Presenting Montesquieu and Mulley' s Circus for Restless Children"

There's a faint bell chime and a dim spotlight that grows brighter. It shines on the older gentleman who has mounted the white horse. He tips his top-hat at me with one hand and holds a flaming ring with the other. I watch the beasts jump through the hoop, their fur barely missing the fire. The leotard dressed women are wrapped in silk fabric ropes which descends somewhere from the striped tent roof. I watch them contouring their bodies into geometric forms- rising and falling with the movement of the silk. One of them looks to me and gives a dark red grin. She descends to me with an extended arm.

I reach out a hand to brush hers, but instead, she whisks me with her- high into the air- high above a crowd of cheering onlookers in the center of the arena.

I cling to the silk, but I feel it slipping through my fingers.

I yell out as the wind rips through my nightgown and shut my eyes as the burgundy floor of the circus arena draws closer.

I awaken to find myself on my bed, alone in the room.

The storm has receded.

What is left is only a light pattering of rain and the scent of candle smoke.

# BABIES DROPPING FROM THE SKY

## ROSALEEN LYNCH

'Stand there,' I tell her, pointing to the spot of chewing gum stuck to the ground between us. 'And don't look up, it'll make you move. Did you do what I said with the bassinet?'

She nods 'yes', in that terrified look of wanting to believe but can't. No use telling her that it doesn't matter if it's a piano or feather falling from the sky, the weight won't decide how it falls, only resistance does.

She will look up. She will want to know what's coming. And she will step back. She's programmed to. Something falling on us gets this reaction. Even if it's a baby. We recoil.

And she does. And I've to grab the edge of the bassinet at the right time, so she rocks forward and back to have the baby drop into it as I let go.

I already had four at home. I'd hung on too long. But this one attached on impact. It's a tightly woven bassinet, and the woman did not let it go.

You ask, 'What if no one's there?'

There always is. That's the trigger. That's not the hard part. It's getting women to believe.

# SPEED TRAP

## RAE THEODORE

He's a wanderer

Slow

Not slow and methodical

Only slow

One speed above still

A notch above nothing

Long limbs loose

Aloof

Two hundred and six bones engaged in a giant shrug

A waste, I think

All of that youthful energy could power a small city

or light up the night sky if he sold it to the stars

Instead, he wanders

Here

There

Couches

Chairs

I wonder whether it matters where he is or where he's
going

He likes to fix bikes

This is his thing

Loosen

Tighten

Pump

Perpetual pit stops

Still, he doesn't seem to be going anywhere

The slowness is a blanket he wraps around himself,

probably for protection,

but what do I know?

I don't wander

At least not enough

I'm always in a hurry, living life in a rush

My strides are purposeful

My goals for each day printed on a whiteboard on my desk

This, too, is protection

The unrelenting doing

Armor forged from tasks, appointments, errands, deadlines

"The Hustle," the pill bottle would say

# THE WEIGHT OF THIS SAD TIME WE MUST OBEY

## LAURA CELISE LIPPMAN

Remains of the dead,

in the abandoned wreck of immigrants

were laved by the weedy tide

that coiled and surged

among the ferny cove;

Its bloody cargo

thrashed and heaved

onto barnacled rocks.

Some kind of shadow was throwing itself

across the negatives

marking our age.

# HONEYMOON DRESSING

## MAUREEN MANCINI AMATURO

Day one of married life shed no light at all on married life. Reality check: we were not going to wake each morning and leave for Italy.

The first day after our wedding, I still felt single, as if exhausted from a big-night bar crawl instead of my own wedding reception. That morning, my biggest concern was what to wear on the plane. I had planned to wear a black, denim, maxi dress, but before I left the office two days before my wedding, as I was hugging everyone and waving bye and collecting wishes and congratulations, my Creative Director's last words to me threw a wrench in my line-up. She said, "Don't wear black on your honeymoon."

That last day in the office, I was in a hurry to catch my commuter bus and get out of Manhattan and home to the hundred or so wedding details I had to address, so I didn't take the time to ask why. I fretted over my affinity for wearing black all the way from midtown's Port Authority, locally known as Port Atrocity, to New Jersey. While waiting for my bus, I re-evaluated my fashion identity. Everything I own is black. Open my closet, and it's like stepping into a cave. There's security in black and mystery, sophistication, elegance, neutrality, and a metropolitan-ness, and aren't I all of those things? And I live in Manhattan, where everyone wears black so that the streets seem to be crowded with shadow people. What's wrong with black? I looked at the several hundred people shuffling and running by me on the bus platform. Ninety percent of them were wearing black. The other ten percent, wearing pastels, were obviously tourists.

Trapped in traffic within the smoggy, dark, exhaust-filled, tiled walls of the Lincoln Tunnel beneath the Hudson River, I couldn't escape the throbbing thought my Creative Director had planted. The always-uncomfortable ride home on a packed, rush-hour bus, sitting crushed against the window, my shoulders rounded forward, several tote bags and packages piled on my lap, and another commuter–dressed in black, by the way–squished against my left side, was even more uncomfortable. I was not only miserable physically in that inhumane seat over the front wheel fender that forced me to have my knees bent up into my chin, but I was in mental anguish. As a person who knocks on wood regularly, I did not want to tempt fate by ignoring my Creative Director's warning. *Don't wear black? But I'm Italian. I'm New York City. I'm in the fashion industry. Everything I own is black. Even my tooth brush is black.* I wondered if it would be bad luck or a taunt to fate if I wore the black maxi. Did it have anything to do with widow? I couldn't even go there.

Superstition won. Once I got home, I intended to dive deep in to my closet, in the back corner where I keep the non-black clothes, and pull out the fuchsia floral on white fit-and-flare and ball up the black denim. I really meant to switch dresses. Really. But our DJ lost my playlist. Two guests cancelled. A friend was coming to drop off the dress she made for my little flower girl. I still had to make my veil and headpiece, and when I looked in the mirror that night to wash my face, my nose looked particularly big. I forgot to switch dresses. All I can say is that when I was getting dressed the first married morning of my now married life, I put on a black maxi dress, and we boarded the plane for our honeymoon in Italy. To hell with omens. I say that now, but truth be told, my brain itched all the way across the Atlantic wondering if I had made a mistake wearing the black dress. Trying not to let all the blue jeans and beige sweaters, all the khaki pants and plaid shirts sitting in the cabin taunt me, there I was–newly married, thirty-thousand feet in the air, wearing black. I worked my newly-wed heart into a frenzy trying to tame my thoughts all the way to the Marco Polo Airport in Venice.

Apparently, if wearing black on your honeymoon was a thing, it passed me by that day. I am now married thirty years, living in an enchanted New York suburb–though less than forty miles out of Manhattan, in personality, it might as well be on the moon, but that's another story–and I still wear black. Daily. Being a full-time working mom with a daily commute to Manhattan, I can't say I have the time to know my neighbors on an intimate level, so it was a bit of an eyebrow-to-hairline moment when two different parents at two different times approached me on the rare days I took off to be at my kids' school. They both asked, "Why do you always wear black?" I didn't know them. They didn't know me. Because of our work schedules, I was rarely there, and most parents at school thought my husband was a single parent as he was the one usually taking our kids back and forth to school.

For all those school parents knew, I could have been in mourning, or wearing black might have been a religious thing, or I could have been a spy. Since no one had ever asked me before, the first time someone asked, I had to take a minute to form a proper answer for this person I had never met. "I wear black because they haven't invented anything darker yet." Whenever I gave that answer, the person who had asked looked perplexed, nodded with a semi-smile, eyes squinting, connection fading as if he or she had fallen into the void of the black top and skirt I was wearing. The reactions didn't surprise me. After all, one person had little whales embroidered on his canvas belt. The other had anchors on her sneakers. I was in my usual—long black skirt, black tee-shirt, red lipstick (yes, even in the afternoon.) If fashion were any indication, it was a sure thing that we weren't going to connect. That became my go-to answer for future curious suburbanites.

When it comes to both my husband and black clothes, it's 'til death do us part. And since I haven't been shopping in Heaven yet, who knows? I might still be buying black in my next life. Death, like marriage, can take the girl out of Manhattan but can't take the Manhattan out of the girl.

# NIGHTS

## DAVID RICCHIUTE

His body drained from the night before, he shirked on cartons packed with product and dozed in an oversized dumbwaiter-lift. He'd worked—he had—to get things done, then shirked the rest of the grueling shift, his body run-down from sleepless nights planning to arrange clandestine plots to manage the winter cold. End of the shift, he walked through snow to the parking lot. Others rushed to get home quick—meager homes, but still. He did not rush. He sat in the car with his hands by his side with all that was his in the trunk.

# HONOR

## C.D. FRELINGHUYSEN

I did good, I was an American boy: I forged my D's into B's, blooded my penknife on frogs. Tantrums every year until they got me a rifle. I pushed Sherri down in the backseat. Led her panties over the skeptical crest of her knees. Stood her up at prom. Loyal to my scumbag friends until they crossed me. Under a whitewashed trellace I dictated my boilerplate vows and cued "My Girl" from rented speakers on scuffed parquet. I Skyped her from Tikrit, then later from Walter Reed, spoon-fed rage to my choking bedbound heart 'til its hue matched the badge.

Discharged to the B-roll life. I traded my tank for a Wal-Mart cart armored with tampons and gels. Teen-proofed our mortgaged mailbox with plywood, stared dumb at the harvest moon, drunk drove down country lanes and killed more deer that way than with the gun. Strange noises from the cellar. An heirloom bookshelf that we filled with CDs and magazines. In perfect bliss we accrued reward points.

Then, I'm stricken with the classic symptoms: marital contempt, moral dissolution, desperate water sports. And on cue, a new secretary appears, clutching a binder to her chest. For two years I seethe until my breakthrough: that it can't be a mid-life crisis at thirty but instead my True Self desperate for expression.

Having surpassed my mental constraints, I redouble my vices, index their correspondent princes, and conjure them in the cellar: Bezaliel, Gadreel, Semyaza. They hand me the standard blood contract and a Band-Aid.

By trimester two I'm folding the secretary at the waist. Lurid days, lurid days: forgetting which gift earrings are whose, Tide penning crimson off my collar, massaging Sherri's swollen feet. I find quotations by famous men who define genius as the ability to maintain contradictory truths. Obsession and Despair. Beauty and Reason. All these famous men were cheaters.

It ends too suddenly. She and I are sniped by telephoto at the Seascape Lodge. I salute the P.I. leaning out his cigar-fragrant Buick.

I kick open the front door. "Honey, I'm home!" On the set and waiting dinner table, two candles are red spidering coins. The ghost in the wall wails. Sherri's eerie silhouette rises from the corner chair. With a glance I catalogue the contents of the knife block.

She hurls the pot roast on the floor. Plates detonate on the wall. I say bad words. She says that one thing I've asked her not to ever say. I gauge her neck's circumference. She steps up to my fist, daring me to do it. Instead I break; I deploy weeping and promises, while she tosses my clothes onto the lawn and kicks me out into a duplex. I never unpack, waiting for a quick reconciliation after a double barrel of counseling and church.

But she's not through. She flatters at custody court and

cuts her hair short. I tell my lawyer to tell her lawyer to tell her that it looks great. She gets a Pell Grant and begins seeing a guy who is taller and sweeter than I. She parades him around town. He hires ugly babysitters and takes her to film festivals, lantern-lit piers, and hot air balloons over meadows: real screensaver dates. Semyaza offers to banish him to Jupiter; I decide that would be passive-aggressive.

The ghost has followed me to the duplex. From the attic, night after night, comes the sound of a shambling man. In my tub I kneel in the scalding spray, pressing together sundered halves of soap.

One night I wait for them in my car. I bang my palms on the wheel when they kiss on the stoop and go inside for more. When the bedroom light goes off I get out and whale on the door and she emerges with a bat and swings at my throat. In her eyes is hate unsoftened by history. Now, she was through with me.

Semyaza on my shoulder asks what I want to do, what topless towers I'd have burned. I tell him instead to take me home and tuck me in, and to check my closet for the monster.

After I depart, after she dismisses her boyfriend, pays the sleepy sitter and puts the colicky baby to bed, assesses the damage I've done to the door, takes off her borrowed dress and her makeup in her dead mother's mirror; after she takes a Tylenol, sets her alarm, and lays down her weary head, the holy spirit visits upon her.

Hellmouths have opened in my master bath; specters bellow at me all night. Each morning I discover a new brand on my flesh, another rotted molar. Semyaza takes my measurements for the iron maiden and calls his wife, telling her he'll be home soon.

The next time I see Sherri is on Pay-Per-View, knocking out the champ at the MGM, while archangels blare Conti's trumpets from the turnbuckles. She pins a barrister wig over her bangs, slams her hands on the bench and catches the star witness in a lie. She cuts into the silent alarm and cracks the safe and gets away with the letters of transit and sells them both. She traces the call to *inside the house* and without a stunt double, leaps in slow-mo with a crossbow and nails the Dracula in the heart.

One day, I'm frying eggs at Waffle House, when someone taps me on the shoulder. It's Sherri -- in a black suit, black gloves. She's got some action planned downtown, but her driver's a no-show. Would I fill in, handle the scanners and radio?

I know how this ends: in jail or the morgue. But I will do this one last thing for her, my beloved: I won't snitch.

# VULGAR AND OFFENSIVE

## W. T. PATERSON

When my mother lost her second husband, I didn't know how to feel about it. She had eloped and sold my childhood house after I moved to the city to try my hand at acting, all of my non-essential belongings sold at a yard sale. The cash came in a birthday card from the new address, and that's how I found out. She still lived in the same small lake town of Clearview, Oregon, but just a few streets over. Clearview is the type of place where people either got out, or they didn't, and there I was moving back in with her.

We had beers together, that second husband and me, Thanksgiving and Christmas the same year watching action movies on late-night cable. That was it. Sitting in his house, my mother already asleep, the man's pale glowing face like a ghost, he looked already gone, never really there. It didn't make sense, but somehow I knew that was all we'd ever have together. Come the next fall, he landed pneumonia and choked to death in his sleep from the fluid in his lungs.

My mother offered the sectional couch in the first-floor sunroom. It folded out into a stiff queen bed and pointed at the unused flat screen by the glass door. Up the creaking stairs was the master bed and guestroom, but I wasn't allowed to stay in the guestroom in case my sister came home. She'd been gone longer than I'd been in the city. And when I say gone, I mean no one knew where she was.

The sunroom had more windows than wall space. Bamboo curtains rolled at the tops of the glass, it was an effort to get them all down. My first night there I didn't bother and then couldn't shake the feeling of being watched. I pulled the thin comforter over my head too afraid to look out the dark windows fearing a face staring back. I stayed that way until morning. When I got out of bed, I caught my mother's nosy neighbor—an older woman with wild, witchy hair—watching me change from the window in her kitchen.

~ ~ ~

"I want you to get a job," my mother said. She came downstairs in a bathrobe and thick glasses. In her mind, a job would keep me out of the house during the day, and home at night to keep an eye on things. She spoke with that disconnected affect of some bygone era as if finding work was as easy as asking for a job. She said, "ask for the manager and shake their hand. Smile. Wear a tie."

The grocery store called me *overqualified*.

"Eggs go on the bottom," I said, "bread on top. An idiot could do this job."

The hiring woman shrugged and said no thanks. She turned and walked behind the special-needs bagger stroking his hair like a cat. The boy smiled. I left wishing I'd chosen a better wording.

The sandwich shop near the highway didn't bother with an application. Instead, the owner asked if I knew the difference between salami and capicola.

"That's what's standing between me and an $8 an hour job?" I asked, and the man pointed at the door. That's the thing about loneliness, it turns people into wolves and when we see each other, all we want to do is battle it out to see who has it worse.

The only place that offered me anything was the local movie theater, the one without stadium seating or digital projectors, the type that played movies from reels of film, and seeing how I wasn't in high school, it didn't feel like a victory. The operating manager was a girl named Jenni that I'd gone to school with, someone who'd been friends with my sister. She still lived in town, still wore sugary perfumes and cherry flavored lip-gloss, still kept her hair in a high ponytail. During the interview she told me that she had plans to one day leave and never come back, but to keep that between us. Then she looked at me like she wanted to ask something and I knew what it was before she found the words.

"Any updates?" she asked. I shook my head no, struggling to breathe, pushing dark thoughts out of my mind.

We went outside to continue the "interview" and Jenni lit up a smoke. She offered me one, but I waved it away to focus on the rumble of the distant highway, of people doing things, going places, leaving and returning.

Jenni lived at her parent's lake house and still threw ragers for high school kids when her folks left town. She told me how every spring they dragged the lake and how, if she was lucky, they found a body or two of some missing person. The town kept it quiet, but it was almost always a kid from another county, or a family man swollen and bloated, crushed by impossible debt.

"When can I start?" I asked. Jenni burst out laughing and put her hand on my chest.

"Whenever you want," she said, and popped a piece of mint gum into her mouth to mask the bitter smoke.

~ ~ ~

That night, I called my buddy Jorge in the city to vent.

"Always room for you at the inn," he said, and I could hear the long drag and exhale of a cigarette. Jorge was good that way, he gave you his attention so as long as something occupied his hands. He was the type of guy that stood outside of liquor stores in a leather jacket, sickly hair slicked back, ripping through smokes, waiting for people with a certain kind of look.

"Nah, straight and narrow," I said. The television on mute, flashing images reflected off of the dark windowpanes around me, swallowing me, taunting me. The woman next door, my mother's neighbor, drew her thin red curtains and undressed against the glow, her naked, ghostly silhouette both distant and present.

"Ain't no such thing," Jorge said, then wished me well. I told him I'd be in touch if things changed. When I stood to unfurl the bamboo shades, I jumped at the sight of my own body reflected back. It looked like I was outside next to the woman's window staring into the room of which I stood. In my white shirt, I, too, looked ghostly and distant.

~ ~ ~

My mother went to bed at the first hint of darkness and rose with the touch of first sun. She rapped on the glass sunroom door and asked what time I started work, then went into the kitchen to prepare breakfast.

"Not until 2:00 PM," I grumbled, rising out of bed to the smell of cooking English muffins. She must have thought I was lying because she opened a newspaper to see what time movie showings started. There were a few at noon, but she said nothing about it. The kitchen floor had checkered black and white tiles like a 50's diner.

"My hope for you was the grocery store," she said, re-folding the newspaper. It was clear she'd been crying. Her thick glasses did little to hide the pink swelling of her lids. "The news did a story on that bagger, the one with retardation."

"You shouldn't say that, Ma," I said, rubbing my face where the imprint of a couch pillow ran three lines from jaw to scalp.

"He puts notes of encouragement in people's bags. Little daily affirmations. Isn't that cute? I got one that read *any day above ground is a good day*," she said. Then she paused and looked out into the small backyard like she had seen something, but when I looked, it was just an old wooden swing blowing from a branch in a tree in a different neighbor's yard.

"You don't say," I said, and yawned.

"What do you think of that story?" she asked. Her eyes looked hopeful when she turned to me, like a cartoon character falling in love.

"I think it's vulgar and offensive," I said, folding my arms across my bare chest. The central air hadn't kicked on and the room stirred with chills. "They wouldn't have done that story if he wasn't special needs. They're pretending we're all the same. But we're not all the same. The story wouldn't be special if we were the same, and so they're calling more attention to the one thing they want us to look past. I mean, if I dropped notes into stranger's bags they'd phone the cops."

"Oh," my mother said, and sat on a chair looking at the refrigerator. She didn't move. She sat there breathing. I wanted to reach out and touch her, hug her, to ask for my mother back, but the English muffins popped, smoking and charred around the edges.

~ ~ ~

My first day at the theater was exactly what I'd imagined. Sweeping popcorn off the sticky floor after a show let out, hauling trash bags to the dumpster in back, learning the POS at the snack bar from a shag-haired high school hockey player who took one look at my body and asked how much I benched.

"Ain't no way you got this job because you *wanted* it," he said, flexing his broad shoulders through the maroon employee polo. "What's the score?"

"No more questions," I said, but the kid pestered me for the rest of the shift with anecdotes about winning the big game, or locker room mishaps, or how one day, he was going to be alone with Jenni and confess his true feelings even though she was older. He said he'd almost done it once at a party, but took too many tequila shots and lost his nerve.

With an hour left in the shift, paperwork done, all duties learned, my future laid out like a movie reel in theater three, another kid came in to take over concessions. The shag-haired hockey player ribbed him for a while, and then clocked out.

"That guy is the worst," the new kid said. He reached into the popcorn machine and grabbed a fistful. He leaned against the freezer and tossed pieces into his mouth. "Name's Greg," he said, wiping a palm across his gut and extending a buttery hand.

"Riley," I said, and didn't shake. Across the room I saw my mother walk in and buy two tickets from Jenni up front. She stumbled in a daze to the dark entrance of a theater like her movements were pre-planned, an animatronics human running the programmed motions. If she saw me behind the snack bar, she didn't acknowledge, so I followed from a distance into theater two and watched as she laughed at the talking dogs, wept at the singing birds, and cheered for the dancing pig as though a child, a little girl, might be sitting next to her. When the credits rolled, I ducked into the lobby. My phone lit up with an incoming call. It was my mom.

"What time do you think you'll be home tonight?" she asked. I watched her walk outside as she waited for an answer, phone pressed to ear like nothing in the world existed, not even me.

"Soon," I told her, and she asked that I lock the doors before bed.

Jorge said he was curious about the woman next door.

"People like watching, and being watched," he said, sucking smoke into his lungs. "You know better than anyone."

"Maybe I'll give her a show," I said into the phone, and Jorge laughed. When the conversation ended, the sun had just started to set. Streetlights clicked on to push back the creeping dark against the tall pines along our quiet street. My mother went to bed and before long her nasally breaths turned rhythmic and deep. Jenni texted a picture of herself standing over a stove making pasta without a shirt, bright blue bra center frame. Sauce dripped from her chin to her chest. She wrote *Cooking mishap! Again! LOL!* The wolf in me began to howl, so I walked up the creaking steps past my mother's bedroom and stood in the door of the empty guestroom. The lamp next to the bed was turned to the dimmest setting, the lampshade painting the room orange and purple. I took off my shirt and sat on the edge of the bed wondering what it would be like to feel my face on the pillow, to see if it still smelled like my sister. Next to the closet stood an almost-full CD tower, the lettered spines bleached by the sun. An oval mirror like a ship's port hung on the wall. Fuzzy white slippers poked from beneath the bed. I didn't realize I had started crying until I held the phone up and snapped a selfie, my skin shining purple and orange. Still, I sent the picture with the caption *cold, empty bed* thinking it was sexy and suggestive. Jenni didn't respond.

The light from the sunroom spilled into the side yard where pine needles scattered the lawn and shadows loomed like waiting fingers to snatch away sleepers. I wondered what my mom felt when her second husband choked to death and she had to sit by watching, helpless.

From the guestroom window, something moved outside. I knelt by the sill. My mother's nosy neighbor tip-toed from shadow to shadow, peeking through the sunroom window. Her wild, witchy hair caught the light. Her thin nightgown moved in the breeze. I felt cold for her. She looked up into the glow of the guestroom and I stood, my upper body filling the window. The woman ran back inside her home and turned off the lights. By the time I went downstairs into the sunroom, I got the sense that she wasn't asleep, that she was waiting in the dark for something, for me, for the chance to glimpse a life that was not her own.

That first year in the city, I blew my money on acting classes with has-beens and took three low-wage jobs to stay afloat until I met Jorge and learned there were other, more profitable ways to make a living.

If the woman wanted a show, I'd give her a show and maybe we'd both feel validated. I turned off the light and slid into bed without drawing the shades. On the cusp of sleep while the creeping sensation of being watched tickled across my flesh, for a moment, I thought I heard the sound of creaking stairs.

~ ~ ~

A few weeks into work, Greg told me about an upcoming vacation.

"Flying to Las Vegas," he said, filling his travel mug with soda from the fountain. "I have a friend out there."

The popcorn kettle hummed ready. I filled the inside with kernels and oil waiting for the tiny explosions to spill over and flood the case.

"Must be a good friend," I said. "Vegas is pricey."

"We've actually never met. Just online," Greg said. "We're both gamers."

The popcorn wasn't popping so I put my fingertips against the kettle to make sure there was heat. The metal vibrated, cool to the touch. Greg leaned over and jostled the plastic coated power chord. The kettle hummed louder and inside of a few seconds, the kernels went off like fireworks.

"Maybe rethink your trip," I said, staring at my reflection in the glass popcorn case.

"He's not some weirdo. Besides, if he is, I can take care of myself," Greg said with the unearned confidence of youth, the untested swagger of comfort, the naïve belief that the world was fair and just. When I looked at him, I knew that when he came back, if he came back, he wouldn't be the same kid.

Jenni pulled me into the break room and sat me down at the round table.

"Today is your thirty day review," she said, and opened a binder. She ticked a bunch of boxes and closed it. "You pass."

"Ok," I said, and stood to leave.

"Wait. Talk to me for a sec. I'm a little starved for conversation that isn't about seventh period social studies," Jenni said, and reached across the table for my hand. She looked like she knew something, like she wanted to tell me something but didn't know how. Her hand on my hand, her lotion-lathered skin across my dry mitts, it was the closest thing to intimacy I'd felt in years. Around us were framed posters from blockbuster movies and an ancient refrigerator with a printed schedule to the freezer door.

"I barely sleep anymore," I said, and closed my eyes. I squeezed her hand.

"Same," Jenni said. She walked around the table and hugged me sideways, her head on my chest, torso against my ribs. Her hair smelled like nicotine. It reminded me of my sister after she met her ex Rob in the months before her disappearance.

"Come over tonight. After work," I said, and Jenni squeezed tighter. The shag-haired hockey player walked in and saw us standing there, his eyes filling with hurt until finally saying the delivery guy needed the manager's signature.

When I went to drive home that night, one of my tires mysteriously had no air so I waited for Jenni to lock up. We drove in her car with the windows down so she could smoke, and I breathed the cool air's thick smell of damp woods and evergreen.

~ ~ ~

My mother was asleep. I drew all the shades but one and unfurled the bed. Jenni told me not to get any funny ideas, even though she was under the covers before I was. We turned the lights off, kept the TV on, and said nothing to each other. The neighbor's silhouette drifted between windows. Close to dawn, neither of us asleep, I broke the silence.

"Where would you go?" I whispered.

"Anywhere," Jenni said, and for that split second, I felt like my sister might still be alive, somewhere else, anywhere else but here. Jenni ran her hand up my leg. She kissed my mouth, the taste of ash thick on her tongue. She kissed my chest. Without meaning to, I slipped into the sweet comfort of sleep. When I woke up, she was gone and my mother paced the kitchen.

"Sometimes," the woman said, looking into the backyard, "I can still hear her voice."

~ ~ ~

A tow truck came to change the tire on my car, even though I swore up and down that I could do it myself. Jenni said that since it happened on the movie theater's property to an employee, their insurance covered it, and why not let someone else do the work?

A guy with a long beard, thick arms and chest and legs with a solid, round gut, jacked up my car and puffed away at a cigarette. Sometimes, I felt like the only person in the world who didn't smoke. The shag-haired hockey player watched with arms crossed from the ticket booth.

"My folks are away for the weekend," Jenni said. "Let me cook you dinner." She hooked a finger through my belt-loop and pulled me into her, our crotches colliding, like my falling asleep cranked up the volume on whatever she thought was going on between us.

"Can you see the lake?" I asked.

"Wide-open view," she said, and then suddenly stopped. She started to say something, her neck making groans and clucks like the beginning of words, but she held a cigarette to her lips and sucked down smoke to quiet the sound of whatever it was she needed to say.

"All set," the tow-truck driver said, and got back into his car before I had the chance to kick him a twenty.

~ ~ ~

My mom came in again that night, this time asking for two tickets to a war movie. She walked through the lobby like she wasn't actually there, like she was floating, like the world was a dream that she could wake up from at any time. I followed her into the theater and sat three rows behind watching her watch bombs go off, and planes zoom by, and soldiers fall into bloody piles. When moments got intense, my mother leaned over to shield the eyes for whoever she thought was sitting next to her.

The movie ended. I hurried back to the snack counter.

My mother exited to the lobby and saw me leaning against the popcorn machine. She froze, then looked at the door, then back at me. She eyed the candy in the glass. I said nothing. Then, she left, and I went into the theater to sweep up knowing full well there wouldn't be anything left behind.

At the end of the shift, I called to say I was going out to eat.

"Lock up when you get in," she said. I heard the television on in the background like she was waiting for me downstairs in the sunroom, and I wondered if maybe she had something to tell me. I imagined the bamboo shades still coiled at the top of the dark glass panes.

~ ~ ~

Jenni's parent's house sat on a plot of land overlooking the town's lake. No close neighbors save for crooked white birch trees and looming pines. A dirt road led to a gravel driveway, which led to a wrap-around wooden porch with loveseat swing and rocking chair. The dark water sparkled and stretched into the sky. Crickets chirped. The air sat heavy in my lungs rich with the turnover of life, of decay, of new life.

Inside, the open floor plan blended kitchen with sitting room with dining room. Stairs lifted to a second story where a library loft looked over the sitting area. Large glass windows faced the water. Smaller windows faced the surrounding woods.

I sat on the couch. Jenni dimmed the lights and my reflection faded into the sparkling dark of the lake.

"What are you hungry for?" she asked, straddling me. She shoved her fingers into my hair and I smelled the sugary perfume on her neck, the recently applied cherry lip-gloss, the stale smell of nicotine on her shirt.

"What if who I am, and who you think I am aren't the

same person?" I whispered. She pushed her pointer finger against my lips until my head pushed into the back cushion. I imagined high school parties where kids drank from red cups, yelled over each other, made drunken bets about skinny-dipping in the lake. I thought I heard gravel crunching outside, the wandering ghosts of all of the parties I never went to.

"I had such a crush on you in high school," she whispered and bit my ear. I put my hands on the sides of her legs. She slid the shirt over my head and tossed it to the floor. Then she took off her own shirt. She bent forward so that our foreheads touched while she wiggled out of her work pants, and then straddled me again until so much of her skin pushed against so much of mine and I felt safe. We hadn't kissed yet, not properly.

I hugged her, squeezing my fingers against her back, digging my face into her shoulder wanting to collapse inside whatever this feeling was. She ran her hand down the side of my face until her fingers wrapped my throat. She squeezed tight enough that it hurt to breathe. I relaxed into it.

The gravel crunched again. I glanced outside and through the dark pane of glass, I saw the face of the shag-haired hockey player looking in.

Jenni felt my body jolt, and when she looked, she saw him too. She screamed. Still in my pants, I stood up and ran outside.

"Hey!" I called after him, the crunch of his sprinting steps disappearing into the dark.

"I had to know!" he shouted back. I couldn't see him, but his voice sounded wounded, angry, hurt. Then, he was gone entirely.

"Little perv," Jenni said, phone in hand ready to call the cops. "I should kick his fuckin' ass."

~ ~ ~

Jenni said she didn't want to stay alone that night, so I told her to come back to my place. She did and when we got home, she went to the bathroom on the first floor. The vent kicked on and standing in the kitchen, I heard her crying.

In the sunroom, I folded up the bed and drew all shades but one. The woman next door's shadow moved across a window. The vent still on in the bathroom, I slid out of my pants and stood naked in the light, erect. The window looked like a pane of glass, the type of glass in the rooms where Jorge brought me, where I put on the rubber horse mask and played with myself while people dropped coins into slots, each one worth $100. Two-way mirrors. I never saw the people watching me, didn't need to, except for once when a lighting rig malfunctioned. It was my second year in the city. No acting gigs had panned out except for this and the money was bank. Jorge took ten percent and we both lived like kings. When that lighting rig snapped, I saw the people behind the glass, the old men with kidney spotted faces, the boozy women with too-large lips, the creeps in coke-bottle glasses and sweaters with thin hair, and in the final booth, I thought I saw my sister's ex Rob. I couldn't be sure, the rubber horse mask obscuring my vision, but I was also sure. He was with someone else. I didn't see who. It didn't feel like my sister, but I've replayed it a thousand times over. I moved home four days later to a house that wasn't mine, to a mother that wasn't the person I'd left behind.

Knowing the neighbor watched from the window in the kitchen, I pulled and stroked, tensing and relaxing, beating and flexing. Slow, then fast, then round, then forward. My chest tightened. The kitchen light clicked off into the red glow and I saw the woman's wild, witchy hair silhouetted against the glass. When I let loose, it shot across the room and onto the bamboo shades, the couch, and my pillow.

The bathroom vent turned off and the door clicked open. I fell to my knees and waited. Jenni found me on the floor, saw the shades, the couch, the pillow, and stepped back into the dark hall.

"I thought you loved me," she said. When I looked at her, she held a trembling cigarette to her lips, but didn't light it. Then, as if she hadn't seen what she saw, as if the last thirty seconds didn't exist, she walked into the sunroom and asked what I wanted to watch. She pulled cushions off the sofa, unfurled the bed, and laid out the comforter. I crawled next to her. She kissed my cheek. And that was the end one thing, and beginning of something else.

All of the lights in my mother's neighbor's house had gone out.

~ ~ ~

We're still dating, Jenni and me. Real dates, too. Dinners, walks through the woods, nights in. I met her parents, and having Jenni around gave my mother a reason to try again, to stop drifting and start anchoring.

One morning, I found her in the kitchen humming. I'd never heard her hum. Part of me felt her happiness to be something vulgar and offensive, because how could anyone ever be happy? But I sat at the table and listened.

"Your sister loved this song," she said, then whistled the rest.

"Mom," I said, and then froze. I wanted to tell her that I was sorry, that it wasn't her fault, that sometimes good people fall into bad situations without knowing they're bad, which didn't make them bad people, it just made them human. Instead, I said, "I think Jenni is still asleep."

My mother stopped whistling and went back to humming.

Greg never came back for another shift at the movie

theater. Apparently he'd returned from his trip, but that's all we knew.

The shag-haired hockey player quit, and in the spring police showed up because he'd gone missing. His parents were worried. I saw in Jenni's face something envious. I knew she thought he'd gotten out, he'd figured a way.

Just before Memorial Day, the town dragged the lake and pulled out his body all bloated and swollen, his lips blue, his skin milky white. It never made the papers, but Jenni and I watched from her parent's porch, something dark and heavy between us, both of us knowing, neither one of us saying it.

I still work at the movie theater. Jenni enrolled in community college and I took over her role. My mom still comes in, still buys two tickets. I still watch her from a few rows back and I don't know if she knows I'm there, but she must, because one day I turned around in my seat when I felt something familiar and comforting, a certain aura, and found Jenni watching me. It made sense that it wasn't the first time.

All of us in that theater bound together by something unspoken, we sit there watching each other wondering what the other is thinking, curious as to the secrets eating away at our lupine souls, for as long as the movie lasts.

# ODE TO A FALLEN STAR

## MISHAL IMAAN SYED

Stars are an etude.

From earth, we call them every kind of music and
poetry—

But the meter holds steady, not free verse.

Compelled into a sort of

Mechanical synchronicity,

The chamber of a flayed heart forced open and

Its contents stuffed, stifled,

Into the sterile compartment of a

Windup machine.


You accustom yourself, I suppose.

You endure, like clockwork

Harmonies prescribed and orbits proscribed

Deviation jilted back down by the

Glaring press of gravity

Is it any wonder, then

That you took one look

At stars rocked into their indolent languor

By the insistent sway and hiss of time

Took one look, your last of its kind—

And, spurred by the passing smile of a comet's tail

Trailing ice and smoke emancipation

You sputtered into heat, and spun

And fell?


(And was the world so much brighter

When you woke?)

# THE SELECTED MEMORIES OF WALTER COBB

## STEPHEN STRATTON MOORE

It's all so quiet now. These rooms that were once filled with the warm light and boisterous din of the Cobb family – now lie empty and cold, almost skeletal. Mother's floral-print wallpaper, that she specially ordered from New York City, peels from the wall in large curling hunks revealing behind it, a glimpse of some other lifetime – gone and forgotten.

The numerous water spots on the ceiling show the neglect of a long-forsaken tin roof. A rooftop still littered, I would guess, with the remnants of my old broken 45 record disks that I tossed up there, like Frisbees when I had tired of the songs.

"Ra-perts...Lil Drum-Drum Drummerboy"

I can hear a steady drip of water from some far-off corner of the house. It all makes me actually believe that there must be something called *time*. That linier time actually exists...but I know better. However, for the sake of this story, I will play along.

Looking around my old home, I find it almost impossible to imagine the lives that were so wonderfully lived – and yes, endured in this old house. There are subtle reminders of them that only I can see. The rest of those details reside in the fading memories of my two siblings who are still living. It was, indeed, a long time ago.

To be completely honest, I had forgotten much of it by the time I died, but then again, it was the nature of my affliction or perhaps the medication. But now, how my eyes have opened – I can see it all! I know it all! I remember it all! I remember every moment, every kiss, every tear, every taunt, every hug, every slap, like it happened only yesterday. I remember the pity and the fear in the eyes of strangers who looked at me for the first time. I remember the whispered affections of my sister Mary, who looked after me then... and I remember beauty, and I remember love.

"I love my hister! Pah!"

I can see all my countless soul memories: the good things and the bad things that I experienced throughout my lifetime. Some of these memories I will share with you... and some... I will not, for there is no point. Through hindsight, I am also able to see and know the things I was blind to then, providing further meaning and context into my extraordinary life.

To begin with, it was the life that I chose to live, and I'd chosen to live it again for many reasons. As difficult as it was at times, this lifetime has been one of my favorites thus far from both a sentient and consciousness standpoint. In the most basic of terms, it was an exercise in complex simplicity...and yes, purity. I've learned so much from it.

Also, as I 'm sure you've noticed and might be wondering about it, I'm including little bits of my lexicon that I used in life, just for fun! My verbal skills were quite rudimentary, but I did indeed have a unique way of expressing myself.

"Pah! Bod-damit!"

## 1943

I was born the sixth child of the Cobb family of Cobin, Kentucky, on the breezeless evening of June 14th. On that night, before I was even properly swaddled and placed under the warming light, our family doctor advised my mother that I should be taken away, right then and there. The doctor had his reasons, of course. He'd seen this before. Once.

I was not a pretty baby. I had a high, broad forehead, two tiny leaking slits for eyes, and I squalled from the start, like a bear cub with a bellyache. Mother first looked upon me with an expression of affectionate bewilderment for almost a minute. She spoke not a word, then kissed my forehead. She then looked up at the doctor and simply said, "No."

~ ~ ~

I was a surprise. What our neighbor tactfully called "an unplanned blessing." One might have wagered at the time that I was more of a curse. For you see, Mother was well passed her childbearing years when I came along. She was not in any way prepared for me. I have no doubt that in her darker moments, she might have considered sending me away, for the burden of my care was heavy.

It was the crying, I suppose. As a newborn, I cried inconsolably for weeks. In my defense, I had a constant ringing in my ears, my head pounded, and my eyes ached from the bright light. I guess it just took some time for my body to adjust to the living world.

I know it was not easy for her. She had some adjustment pains all her own. She was so heartbroken that nothing she did could soothe me. Hopelessness is a hard thing for a mother to endure. Meanwhile, there were five other Cobb kids who demanded her attention. Also, though unspoken, she knew that Daddy needed her to help run the grocery store. Normal life had to resume at some point.

~ ~ ~

Mother and Daddy took me back to the doctor to seek some kind of relief. The doctor looked me over, prescribed some medication, and recommended that I be kept in a dark room.

Dr. Runyon then called in his nurse to look after me and motioned Mother and Daddy into his office. Curiosity led me to follow after them in my mind. It was as if I were now a fly on the wall, listening in to the speech that he had prepared for them.

"Mr. and Mrs. Cobb, your son, Walter suffers from a genetic condition called Mongoloid Lunacy. There is no cure nor any treatment for it. Furthermore, there is no hope for any cognitive development beyond the age of three in the best of cases. All our scientific studies show that he will not have the opportunity to live any kind of meaningful life, and I can assure you that it would be extremely difficult to attempt to raise him at home. He would be, in essence... a wild child. His life span will be very short. It is my opinion, as your physician, that the most humane action is immediate institutionalization. I strongly recommended this for Walter, as soon as possible, before any further bonding takes place. Honestly, it is in the best interest of all involved, Mr. and Mrs. Cobb. This is the best thing for Walter. This is the best thing for you and the rest of the Cobb family. Mount Grayson is a wonderful facility, and I'm sure Walter will thrive there. I've taken the liberty to set up a visit and tour for y'all."

Mother and Daddy went to Mount Grayson the following weekend. They never spoke again about that visit.

~ ~ ~

That same weekend, my mother's elderly aunt Rella came to stay with us for a little while. I actually remembered her in life. She later showed me that I had a special gift.

She smelled like lavender and sang to me in a soothing high voice, as she rocked me back and forth. She sang an old song from long ago that went, "*Oh-ro, soon shall I see them; He-ro, see them, oh see them; Oh-ro, soon shall I see them; the mist-covered mountains of home.*" Aunt Rella was the one who finally helped me to stop crying… and sleep.

~ ~ ~

I was raised at home, and with time, I became more manageable. Our neighbor babysat me during school hours until Mary came home. She took over the bulk of my daily care through my toddlerhood while Mother and Daddy were working. My other siblings helped out, as well.

My earliest memories were quite happy, filled with daily discovers and wonder. My myopic world was my house and my back yard. They put up chicken wire to keep me in, and it worked for a while.

There was a long line of rose bushes along the back of the house and two huge magnolia trees. With their sprawling branches and broad leaves intertwined together, they shaded the back portion of our yard, creating a bare section of clay that became my favorite spot in the summertime. It was there that I discovered red ants and roly-poly bugs. The ants I didn't like so much, but the roly-poly bugs were, and still are my favorite bugs, except for the praying mantises that lived in the rose bushes and daddy long legs, of course!

~ ~ ~

When I was the six, my parents attempted to put me in school. I made it halfway through first grade, but that was as far as I got before the school officials finally said, "No more."

There were some behavioral issues and several of the other parents complained about me. The principal finally told Mother and Daddy that the school did not have the staff to be constantly watching after me. There was also a letter that stated, among other things, that *Walter is a disruption to the order of the classroom and a hindrance to the proper learning environment of the other students. Surely there are other, more suitable accommodations available to him elsewhere.* There was not.

I remember my last day of school was the final day before Christmas break. The teacher decided to let us do some coloring and passed out dittos and crayons to the children. The ditto spun onto my desk. To me, it was a picture of a pointy-masked robber man with tall crazy hair and bushy eyebrows. I pulled out my black, brown, and orange crayons and went to work coloring the bandit man the best I could. The teacher then collected all the colored pictures and pinned them up above the chalkboard side by side for the rest of the day. *Santa, Santa, Santa, Santa, Santa, Upside-Down Scary Robber Man, Santa, Santa, Santa.* Looking up at that line of papers was the first moment of my life when I realized that maybe – I was different.

~ ~ ~

When I was much older, car rides made me nervous, but as a kid, I loved them. The back seat of our family car was a bouncy, cavernous wonderland and more often than not, I had it all to myself. My favorite thing to do was to press my nose against the cold glass and watch the world pass by.

On one particular ride when I was eight, my sister Mary, Mother, and I were going to the cemetery to place flowers on the grave of a newly-passed neighbor. It was Mary's friend's dad who had died suddenly of a heart attack.

Our car pulled up behind several others that were already parked on the gravel lane. Mother turned to me and said over the front seat, "Walter, I want you to stay close; do you understand me?"

"Opay, Mother." I replied, grasping Mary's outstretched

hand, as we walked over to join the gathering of people. I remember the smell of grass and freshly-turned earth, and I saw a fat lady holding a handkerchief over her mouth. Her middle was jiggling as if she were laughing, but I knew that she was crying. There was a quiet man, who stood off to the side of the gathering, his head was bowed, as if paying his own private respects. He looked lonely.

I don't really remember whether I let go of Mary's hand, or she let go of mine. Mary was distracted by her friend, and I was distracted by the faint music. It wasn't music; it was singing. It was the sound of a woman singing from far away. I took two steps toward it, stopped and looked back. Mary was hugging her friend, and Mother was rubbing the arm of the fat lady, so I knew they were okay. *I'm gonna go see where that pretty music is coming from.*

~ ~ ~

The family story goes that Mother and Mary were momentarily distracted, and I wondered off and got lost somewhere in the big cemetery. Everyone was very worried about me, and they all, even the fat, jiggly lady, split off in every direction to search for me, calling out my name in the twilight.

I was eventually found on the far side of the cemetery, sitting on a newer looking tombstone in the old section. The kicker of the story was that even though I could not read, nor had I ever been to the cemetery before, I was found sitting on the gravestone of aunt Rella, singing a song, or in my case, kind of wailing and moaning. *It was quite the coincidence! What were the odds?*

What do I remember? I knew exactly where I was going. I was never lost, and I had a very nice visit with aunt Rella. Before I was found, she taught me a beautiful old song that she used to sing to me when I was a baby. She told me how proud she was of me, then tousled my auburn hair and whispered, "You will see that God has blessed you,

Walter." Then, she kissed my broad forehead. I was not so sure about the blessing part at first, but after that day in the cemetery, my life did, in fact, change for the better and the worse.

~ ~ ~

From that day on, as if some door had suddenly opened up to me, I was able to see things that other people could not see. More accurately, I could see *people* whom other people could not see. Good people and bad people alike would come and visit me at night.

It was very scary at first, but eventually, I got used to them. With some guidance from the other side, I learned how to identify the good spirits from the bad ones by the color of their light. I also learned how to block the bad ones out, most of the time.

"Hey, Homer, Yup. Nope. Alabambambama?"

Homer was my uncle and my favorite nightly visitor. His light was very pretty. He died in the "Great" war, but he never talked about that. Instead, he'd sit by my bed and tell me stories about how he and Daddy would go fishin' together and climb trees and kiss pretty girls back when they were little boys like me. Homer had lots of stories and more often than not, I'd be asleep before he was done telling them. You know, he could have just told me the same story over and over again, and I would have been happy. It was the sound of his voice, the tambour that I loved. It resonated like the wood of a fine violin when played by a master. He made bedtime fun, and something that I looked forward to every night.

~ ~ ~

The next big moment in my life came when I was sixteen. My sister Mary and my older siblings were well out of the house by then. Mother stayed at home with me at that time. She and Daddy bought me a record player and some

45 rpm records to keep me entertained and out of trouble during the day.

Much like receiving the gift of sight from aunt Rella, it felt like I had received the gift of sound, or more accurately, the gift of music from Mother and Daddy. It was glorious!

It was the tactile vibrations that I loved the most. I always kept my fingers on the little tabletop that the record player sat on. The vibrations of the music went through my fingers up my arm and into my body at the same time the sound waves went into my ears and down my neck. Both of these independent sensations joined in my chest and swirled there for the duration of the song. I can only describe it as pure energy coalescing in me like a sonic galaxy spinning in inner space.

The first five records I got were, "The Tennessee Waltz," "Fernando's Hide-A-Way," "Doggy In the Window," "Shake Rattle and Roll," and "On Top of Old Smoky." I'll let you figure out which of those eventually ended up on the roof.

Entire days would pass by as I played record after record. Moving my body back and forth in my rocking chair and singing along with the music, I practically went to the moon with excitement when Cleveland, a spirit friend who came to a lot of my bedroom dance parties, showed me that there was another song on the other side of the record. Man! Was that a great day. I was so grateful to him; I came up with a special nickname for my good friend,

"B-Side Pleveland, pah!"

~ ~ ~

As the years went by, there were more and more nieces and nephews who came around at Christmas time. The older ones brought me records, sometimes new and sometimes from their own collections. I had developed quite the collection of my own by then with my 45 disks eventually stacked in a single black column in the corner of my room from the counter top to ceiling. The most impressive aspect was the variety of music. I had popular and funny songs, rock-n-roll, Mo-Town, marching bands, folk, show-tunes, even some classical.

"Ra-perts. Hia State Band. Pah!"

In return for the records, I'd entertain my family members with my ability to retrieve a requested song from the middle of the stack. A niece asked me to find "Flying Purple People Eater," and I would run my finger down the column of records to the right spot and pull it out for her, then replace it back to the same place. They'd clap their hands and tell me how amazing I was. I had no idea what the big deal was. It was easy. They called me the human jukebox. I had no idea what it meant, but I liked it.

~ ~ ~

There was definitely something about my affliction that made me sensitive to certain things. Along with my inner joy of music and my heightened awareness of vibration, I greatly enjoyed *Life* magazine. Not in the same way that everyone else enjoyed *Life* magazine. What I loved about it was the smell of the ink and the wonderfully broad pages of thin paper.

When I'd get a fresh one, I'd balance the magazine on the palm of my right hand and bring down my left with a great slap. I would continue this motion until the thin paper began to loosen and separate from the staples. It was the pitch of tearing sound that I enjoyed and the mental image of the individual paper fibers giving way in uneven, jagged edges that simply delighted me. I'd work on a magazine for hours, eventually tearing the loosened pages into ragged strips.

It was all about the vibrations, both tactile and auditory.

The particular frequency of sound created by the tearing of the thin and colorful paper. It was a sound that I think a bee might enjoy, reminding it of the vibration of its fragile wings as it flew from flower to flower.

I can say this:  the living world, as we know it, has everything to do with vibration. Even now, in my pure energy state, I am unable to completely remember all the details. However, in my past carnal state, I was instinctively aware and knowledgeable of all the delicate machinations. I knew then how the physical world functioned. The only thing that I can draw from it now is this:  as human beings, we all love music, for many more reasons than we know. For music is the closest paradigm we can understand that marginally emulates how the physical world manifests itself. All of my singing and tearing of paper was in reverence of this knowledge. Those physical activities paid a simple homage to the vibration of the minute particles that create the temporary illusion – that is us.

~ ~ ~

I sat on a stool at the end of the kitchen counter while mother made a plate for me. Because of my lack of teeth, having lost most of them early in life, my dinners were made up of mostly softer things like mashed potatoes, over-cooked peas, and white bread. My favorite food was fried liver that mother would cut up into tiny pieces for me. I'd suck on the pieces until they were tender enough to chew.

My table manners were not the best, so my mealtime differed from the rest of my family. To begin with, I was completely fine with this arrangement because it meant that I would always get to eat before everyone else. When I was finished with my dinner, everyone else in the house would then sit down together and have their meal. Invariably, I'd feel left out, especially at holiday time when the entire family was there. They would all be talking and having fun without me, and it made me mad, even kind of sad.

There was a louvered door between the kitchen and the dining room that was always propped open against the wall with a rubber wedge. Whenever I got to feeling neglected, I'd run up, swing my arm around the corner, and slam the louvers with my open hand. It made the most satisfyingly reverberating whack that always made me feel better. Over many years of doing this, the three louvers at my arm level were broken out. For some reason, they were never replaced.

For snacks, I liked saltine crackers spread with butter that I'd let melt in my mouth. Sometimes, Mother would set out a dish of salt and pepper for me. I'd lick my finger and dab at the dish until the flavor was gone. For special treats, I'd get to go to the Dairy Isle or as I called it, the *Drive In*. It was a wonderful place!

"Pope! Choplate milp-shape!"

I'd get a car ride and something cold and sweet to eat or drink! Chocolate was my favorite food group. I remember at Christmas time, there were always those holiday boxes of assorted chocolates around the house. I only liked certain kinds. They all looked the same to me, so I took little bites to see if I liked it. If not, I'd put it back in the little paper cup and try the next one. I got yelled at a lot for that, but it happened every Christmas.

~ ~ ~

It's interesting how life can go on for long stretches in predictable ebbs and flows of happiness and discontent. Decades of living can float by within the same known perimeters that we assume will last forever. And then, all of the sudden everything is horribly different. The world that we knew gets turned upside down in the blink of an eye.

It was a late afternoon in the springtime when it

happened. Mother lay on the kitchen linoleum. I could tell that she could not move her body at all, except for her eyes. She looked right at me with tears streaming down her cheeks as if to say, "I'm so sorry, Walter."

It was just us and I panicked, I knew there was something I should do, but I didn't know what. I ran into the other room. Then, I ran back and slammed the louvered door as hard as I could and ran back into the front room. There, I paced back and forth a few times, then ran back into the kitchen.

"Mother, pah. PAH!"

I had no idea how to make her feel better. I knew everything was wrong. This was very bad. I did not know how to sooth her... so I did the best I could. I sat down beside her and began to pat her – her eyes smiled at me one last time and then closed.

I pat her hair for a long time, until Daddy came home. Looking back at it now, what I felt during those hours, must have been what Mother felt when I was an inconsolable newborn. Hopelessness is a hard thing for a child to endure.

"Pah!"

~ ~ ~

The years after Mother passed away were difficult. For long periods, it was just Daddy and me. Honestly, I have to say that he tried his best to take care of me, he really did, but his patience was much shorter then Mother's, and he got mad at me a lot. He never had anything to do with raising us kids, let alone someone like me. He was always at the store during the day when I was growing up, so the situation was new for the both of us.

We each responded to the new dynamic in unhealthy ways. My door slamming increased precipitously, and I decided not to respond when he called out for me. In return, Daddy, feeling disrespected, pulled out his belt and would come hunting me. Thankfully, being as old as he was, he rarely caught me, and that made him even angrier. Somehow, we both survived in this way for almost a decade.

As the Cold War raged on in the world outside our house, another raged within. The family still gathered here at Christmas; my sisters would come and stay with us for a week in the summertime to clean the house, but in between those two events, it was just us.

Thankfully, my brother's family still lived in town, and they checked in on us regularly – enough to keep both of the super-powers from complete self-conflagration.

Mother stayed for a while before she had to cross over to the light. Homer was there to keep me company and help me through the more difficult times when Daddy got too frustrated. There was also the dance party crowd who came around from time to time. I was never really alone, but I was lonely. I remember then; it was like I was constantly waiting for things to get worse, waiting for the other shoe to drop… and finally, it did.

~ ~ ~

Mount Grayson looked quite pretty from the outside with its Gothic architecture and beautifully landscaped grounds, which by the way, you could not see from the inside. One would think that seeing such natural beauty would do good things for the wellbeing of the patients, but as I would soon find out, *patient wellbeing* was never a top priority here. This was certainly not the most pleasant destination for me, but there was no place else for me to go.

Daddy fell and broke his hip. Ironically, he eventually ended up somewhere similar to Mount Grayson, minus the Thorazine and arm restraints. As it was for all the crimes that we committed against one another, we each were given life-sentences in separate prison systems.

~ ~ ~

By malevolent design, my personal illusion of time was deliberately altered that first day at Mount Grayson. Within an hour of my family leaving, I was removed from my nice room and placed in a windowless basement cell that noxiously smelled of fresh paint. It was a bare room with a metal bed bolted to a concrete floor with a commode in the corner. On the ceiling was a cage of fluorescent lighting that vibrated in a minor key and made me want to vomit. Additionally, there were scary noises that emanated from down the darkened hallway outside my room.

Homer and B-Side were there with me, but they warned me that there was only so much they could do. There were bad spirits here with equally bad intentions, so I was most grateful for their company. They protected me from the bad spirits, but they could do nothing to protect me from Terry.

~ ~ ~

The secret program was called Baseline Behavioral Control protocol. All new arrivals were subjected to the process for whatever period of time that it took to create the desired effect. It took longer for some patients than it did for others. Unfortunately for me, I was in the former category.

The patients were placed in a purgatory of sensory deprivation designed to create an existence that was moment-to-moment and more conducive to manipulation. By introducing the patient to manageably, negative stimulation from the beginning, a behavioral baseline was developed and documented that could easily be utilized later as a behavior modifying or disciplinary tool. It was a brilliantly, evil, and equally effective program.

~ ~ ~

After a week, I graduated from BBC, and things normalized. I was allowed back in my good room with the window. I was given back my personal items including my rocking chair, record player, and a few records to play but warned not to play them too loudly, or I'd go back to the basement. That's when I learned how to whisper sing.

That was also around the time I met Maurice. He was nicer to me than the other nurses. He took an interest in me for some reason. I guess he liked the music that I played. He asked me a lot of questions and always stopped by my room when he was on his rounds to make sure I was okay.

"Hey, Walter, what's your favorite song?" or "Hey, Walter, you ever hear of Mo Town? That's where I'm from, Man!" or "Hey, Walter, are you a cool enough to be listening to that song? Slap me some skin now!" I liked Maurice. He watched out for me like Homer and B-Side did, but he was alive. Maurice protected me the best he could. But I never told him about Terry. I never told anyone about Terry. I hated Terry.

~ ~ ~

Maurice was there the last time my sister Mary and her family came to visit me. They talked for a long while, and then she hugged him. Mary invited Maurice along to join us. We all loaded in the car and went to the Dairy Queen. I sat outside in the sunshine with my cousins while she and Maurice went inside to order. I was so happy that day!

"Ice Pream! Choplate Milp-shape!"

~ ~ ~

All the missing pieces of my memory fell into place after I eavesdropped on their conversation inside that Dairy Queen as they sat, waiting on the food.

"I'm not supposed to be speaking to you about Walter, Ms. Mary, but I think something happened to him, something bad that he won't talk about. Don't get me wrong now, Mount Grayson is as safe as society is, but there are some bad apples. Anyway, Walter's been causing problems. I've seen the behavior before. He's holding something in and acting out because of it. It ain't his fault. He don't know what he's doing, but it's starting to become a regular thing. Some of the higher-ups, they want to transfer Walter to our Georgia facility. It's a pretty rough place, Ms. Mary. I just wanted to let you know what's going on. I'll do everything I can to protect him here, but I can do nothing once he goes down there. I got to tell ya, I really like the cuss though. He reminds me of my brother, Alfred. He had the same condition, you know? Al passed away when I was a kid. I guess he's the reason I chose this line of work. Anyway, Walter, he's got some wild taste in music now, but he'll play the Mo Town pretty regular, so he's alright with me!"

~ ~ ~

I guess it was the confidence in Terrence Reginald Wood's eyes that finally set it off. Up to that point, Terry had done whatever he wanted to do to me. When I walked into that commons room that day and saw him standing there, it all just happened. I honestly had no idea of the fearsome rage that had built up and was about to blow. One single, shocking moment, that would eventually prove to be the end of me.

It wasn't all because of him, mind you. My rage was a product of a lifetime of raising myself above all of the folks who had looked down upon me. It was the final human result of a soul who always took the high road... until he didn't. Poor Terry, he was just in the way of it all – the lifetime of repression that released itself upon the world that afternoon.

It was simultaneously the best... and the worst moment of my life when I crashed the Coke bottle over his head. The bottle shattered in an explosion of glass, dark fizzy liquid, and blood. Terry dropped to the floor like a twitching rag doll, the snarky smile still on his face.

"Baaaaaaaaad Pope Pola! Pah!"

To be honest, I was surprised at my strength. I had no idea that I could do that to someone. In thirty seconds, I spanned the entire emotional spectrum – from blind rage to complete elation… and then to raw reptilian fear.

I started to run from the room when two attendants pushed through the door blocking my path. They started to move toward me with their arms out as if to catch me. I panicked and chose the only way out that I had: I crashed through a window, falling two stories to the snow and concrete below.

~ ~ ~

I was out of it from then on – in a twilight state in and out of consciousness. I landed hard on a sidewalk, striking my head and badly fracturing my leg and hip.

My sister Mary came and stayed with me in the hospital. She'd hold my hand and whisper in my ear, even when I wasn't responsive to her. I'd wake up at some odd hour of the night to find her sleeping in the chair in the corner, her coat draped over her like a blanket. She was always smiling, even when she had tears in her eyes.

"I love my hister."

I remember Mary kissing my forehead and cupping my cheek gently. She looked into my eyes, smiled and said, "You sleep, okay? I'll be back in the morning. I love you."

~ ~ ~

I awoke later that night with a feeling of a presence in my room. I opened my eyes and smiled. Maurice was standing awkwardly by my bedside. He was staring at me with the oddest expression on his face. It seemed like it was a long time before he spoke.

"Walter… you know that I love you, right?" Maurice glanced nervously at the door then reached into in his coat pocket and pulled out a three-inch piece of plastic.

"Hey, Walter... What's your favorite song?"

With a practiced flick of his finger, Maurice cleared the air from the needle and expertly injected the entire contents of the syringe into the IV tube. I smiled at him faintly, feeling warmth wash over me and sang the old song. *"Oh-ro... He-ro... Oh-ro... He-ro... Oh... ro... He... ro... pah."*

# TO BE PRECISE

## JAMI WILLIAMS

I started photographing storms the day after I got the call from my brother's oncologist. When Dr. R calls you from his own cell phone, you bargain with the universe with such rapidity that you do not notice the ground falling under your shoes. When Dr. R says hello to you in his lilting, Indian accent, your heart begins to wilt a little. When Dr. R repeats your name more than twice during the conversation, it is perfectly permissible to assume the worst. When you hang up the phone standing in the middle of your driveway around 5 p.m. on a Monday, and the neighbors see you are on your knees wailing like you're at the feet of Christ, they will say nothing. There will be flowers and food on your doorstep each morning. People will wave from doorways, cocking heads in that way that implies they know what is going on and wonder what your family did in the past to bring this curse upon you now. You are the local version of the Kennedy family, minus the Hamptons. No one approaches because you are a monstrous, tentacled, storied sea beast, pulled from the tranquil ocean darkness and left to flail on the ship of fools that snagged you and brought you up. The beast would not intentionally harm someone trying to help it; the beast is merely confused and suffering and trying to breathe.

To be precise: I am the beast.

~ ~ ~

My older brother, John, lives with us now, and I am his primary caretaker. I am not his caregiver; that honor now belongs to my husband. Classic good cop/bad cop. I inherited John when my mother died. John is 52, autistic, and developmentally delayed, however on his paperwork, it says "MR" for moderately retarded. The definition of the word "retard" is simple; the connotations are not necessarily bad. The denotation, when used by a pimply-faced, over-indulged teenager, is like the lick of a whip to my inner ear. The word is both verb and noun; when it is a verb, it is often applied in music, scribed as an instruction to slow the tempo. It gets messier when it is a person, place, or thing. The pronunciation changes from emphasis on the second syllable (reTARD) as a verb, to emphasis on the first syllable (REtard) as a noun. ReTARD, verb. REtard, noun My husband had to intervene once when I nearly punched a small sausage of a woman at Walmart because she asked if John was a REtard.

To be precise: My brother is the verb.

~ ~ ~

John loves my husband because he is the father, brother, co-conspirator, that John has never had. John is simple. He is simple in the way that he puts flags outside on Memorial Day, Flag Day, Fourth of July, Labor Day and Veterans Day. John is simple in that he must purchase bananas at Walmart and saltines at Dollar General, in that order, every Sunday. He is simple in the way that he is innocent. John has never had sex, he has never had a drink of alcohol, he has never hurt anyone, he cannot lie. He is the perfect victim. This is his third round of colorectal cancer, the worst cancer for a simple man. Everything is open for investigation, exposed and explored by a parade of strangers who wear gloves and use their note-taking pens to move body parts out of the way. I, however, do not mention to the doctors that every time my brother gives them permission to look, poke, touch, see, he believes they are miracle workers that will exorcise him of evil. We are told in the Bible that God watches over fools and little children with special care.

To be precise: I am the fool.

~ ~ ~

I wait until after supper to tell him. Monday night is deli pizza night, and John cooks the pizzas. He is the only person in our house who understands our oven like they are both parts of a hive mind. John never under or overcooks the pizza; it is always perfect. After the deli pizza is consumed, I tell him. *John, do you remember the 13-hour surgery you had two years ago when the doctors removed all the soft tissue in your pelvis? Do you remember when those same doctors had to repeat the surgery? They told you that horrendous, ungodly, inhumane procedure, after which you could not sit for three months, meant cancer wouldn't come back for five to seven years? Do you? Good. They lied; there is a mass on your pelvic bone, and they are going to do a biopsy. Do you have cancer? John, you never didn't have cancer. Your margins were positive, even after they removed every single piece of soft tissue in your pelvis, gave you a urostomy on your stomach to go with the colostomy you have dealt with for eight years, and quite literally ripped you a new asshole. No, don't be silly, it didn't grow back. It was always there, just hiding behind your pelvic bone. I know you did everything they said. I know they told you five to seven years. I know you want to walk in the Survivors Lap at the Relay for Life this year... I don't know. I don't know. I don't know times infinity, but I love you, John.*

~ ~ ~

Tuesday morning, the phone rings, and it is the overly friendly, but suitably empathetic scheduling lady from the hospital. She is informing me that John's ultrasound-guided needle biopsy will be next Monday. I thank her and go upstairs to tell John. His first reaction is to the word "needle." All color drains from his face, and he immediately appears shorter, somehow, as if this is bearing down on him with such force that his spine is compressing. I assure him they will anesthetize him. He asks if he must stay the night in the hospital; his voice is higher and pitchy, signaling his fear. I tell him no. I tell him it will be okay. I know that it will not be okay; Dr. R also mentioned the fact that in the last three months, his margins have tripled. I am a liar. I am not simple or innocent. Suddenly, I cannot look at John anymore, cannot watch the same eyes as mine squint in imagined anguish, cannot reconcile the fact that my brother must wear his own excrement on his person, cannot stand that it is not me. I want cancer, hell, yes! I want cancer if it means my brother doesn't have to have it again. I want all the cancer, all the cancers in the world, to crawl in through my tear ducts and pulse through my body. I will martyr myself to cancer; put me on a putrid, rotten, disgusting, filthy cancer cross, wrap me in a purple ribbon, and offer me up in flames. Not because I am a righteous person but because I am a selfish person. I do not want to be me going through John having cancer again. I am not simple or innocent. To be precise: I am a disciple of self-loathing.

~ ~ ~

A storm is pillaring in the west when I walk out to the driveway and get in my car. The Missouri sky screams in a whisper when she is in harm's way. If you watch her, she will carefully offer instruction on what is about to happen to her. She does not fret over storms from the west; she simply hunkers down, waiting for them to overcome her. Storms from the north or the south cause her to panic, and she puts herself away slowly but shaking as if she fears they are not merely passing through. They posit in her an idea that she is terminable, expendable in some way. Right now, she is being sucked into something darker than herself. On the horizon, she is still herself, a prophetess in a luxurious, blue robe with a word for the to-come. But two devil's tongues lick down onto her as if to lap her up into the current of thinly veiled gray moving north. Her sun is shining under the clouds, the trees are skeletons reaching up to grab at her. Above the devil's tongues is a solemn navy blue, the hue of navy blue that means business. The navy blue is substantial, hungry, ominous, and inert. If it is not moved by the wind, then it must be creating the wind. I am moved to stagnancy, fascinated by this thing that is welling up in my heart, this curiosity, this understanding, this poignant realization. I love storms, I love them in the way that a toddler loves pudding... because it is effortless, acceptable, and temporary. How could I love them my whole life and not know them until this throbbing moment? Their thunders whisper my name, their lightning is a beacon, signaling home. I pull over and get out of the car, pushing against the wind to stand up. The navy blue bends in a hospitable smile, revealing what was underneath all of that business.

Death gray, a pallor of insistent strength, splits the navy blue, and the storm speaks. Distance allows it to be a symphony of whispers, the players scurrying to their seats before the maestro lifts the baton. There is a tender line between love and anger; the storm loves this sky. After all, the storm is not territorial; it does not want to stage a coup, does not want to overthrow her country, or take her crown. It is passing through, not invading. There is such resonance in the distinction. The storm cannot help itself. The sky is gone, there is only storm, fallen pillars of black blue and gray cracking open over the sun. I take my phone out and start snapping. I must document this war, this skirmish, this thing happening right now, as darkness fans out, napalm to the spring sky.

John is terrified of storms. As a child, he would whimper when the sky turned dark; he would jump off his bike at full speed, running for the house. Thunder hurt John in some primal way; the timbre of thunder was John's Solfeggio Frequency inverted. Not the noise, but the vibrations hurt his body. Suddenly, I am six years old, and it is April; John's bike passes by me without John, and I can smell rain. The sky is disappearing. I abandon my worm digging and run for the house. John is whimpering as I collect every pillow in the house, tossing them onto my bed. I grab his hand and he grabs mine with both of his. This is a breaking of his own rule; John doesn't enjoy touch. I interpret this as fear. I make him lay down on the pillow bed. I burrito-wrap him in my blanket. I put cotton in his ears. His fear makes him eerily compliant. I sit, my feet on the floor, desperate to catch a bit of his pain. How could we share a mother, share blood, share a two-stick popsicle, and still be so not of each other's ilk? He is an Egyptian tomb, a burial ground of everything with which I am alive; unearthed, and wholly misunderstood. I need to excavate him; even a child can grasp the horror and excitement of the unknown. A sharp strobe of lightning flashbulbs the sky; the thunder rattles the windows, tickles my feet. John is silent. I am terrified. This is a hypothesis, and the if/then of this experiment will most likely end, for me, in either a spanking or a switch. But John smiles up at me, closes his eyes and hums happiness and approval; I have crashed through one side of the tomb, finding riches in making just one connection. I open the window and invite the storm wind to blow in, rain-scented and promising, sprinkling us every now and then, a cold pellet to remind us that this was reality, this pillow-lined burrito bed. To be precise: I am an archaeologist.

~ ~ ~

I stop snapping pictures when my phone vibrates, and I see it is John. Do I know there is a storm coming? Will I be home soon? He's just worried about the dogs, as they tend to get a bit upset when the storms come. I tell him I am on my way; I am a liar. I lean into the storm, the gravel dust spinning around my shins and reminding me that there is pain, always pain to ground me. John will be fine if I am not at home for this storm; there are other souls in the house. There is no more burrito bed; John deals with storms by way of his own machinations now. He is grown up, and he is a child.

Friday comes another storm from the west. Wednesday and Thursday are a mixed bag of questions that I cannot answer. John mowed the yard, John rode his bicycle, John went for walks. John is concerned because the garbage disposal does not work. When I fix the garbage disposal, he is confused because James is the man of the house. John is very much a stay-in-the-lane thinker. I tell him that my fingers are small, and it doesn't hurt me to lay on the kitchen floor. He examines his own fingers, and we stand, palm to palm, for one still moment in the kitchen. He is humming, Mom used to call it purring. He does that when he is content, when conditions are favorable, but he has not forgotten Monday. Will it hurt? Will we leave early? Will we be able to stop at McDonald's on the way home? Yes, yes, and yes, I tell him. There is no need for me to listen to the questions because this is not new to us. When an ailment becomes a routine, there is something so tragically comical about questioning it, or is comically tragic? Does it matter? Will it change things? Can I do this with him? No, no, and no, I tell myself.

With the sun shining and the sky blue, James and I leave on Friday, a justified "just-us" road trip, but I know the temperament of the sky; she is yawning, bored with us. She will invite the storm today, from the west, but offer first a bit of a reprieve, enough of the sun to put some color back into the resurrected world of spring. James needs to talk about allowing John to fight cancer the way he wants to fight. I am not listening, I am cold-hearted and trite, my spirit is turning navy blue around the edges. I watch the low gray clouds tickle the sky's backbone. The storm will drink her; it is not a surrender, it is a rudimentary seduction. The sky is not being invaded, she is allowing passage to this amalgam of heat and cold, this pillaring, stacking of elements that should never meet, that refuse to touch. The refusal will rip at her terra: but she will not hunch over to protect it. She will not put her hand down, cupping over those whose bones ache as the thunder solemnly stumbles across her saturated blue. She will allow it, arrogantly believing she has a choice. She will maintain a specific gravity allowing her to emerge unscathed. She is not courageous, she is a bargain-maker, a traitor. She does not disappear when darkness falls; she becomes the darkness. The sky is a chameleon, a doppelganger who is fixed and staid only in the reality that she will never be stronger than the storm. She is corpulent with confidence that she may offer the appearance of strength by emerging in its passing. She is not simple. She is a liar. To be precise, I am the sky.

# IN THE BELLY OF THE
# CLIMATE CHANGE BEAST

## PATTY SOMLO

Particles of white ash rained from the sky. Flakes resembling old peeled-off paint buried the glass top on the patio table, whitened the otherwise bright rainbow stripes of the plump cushions stretched across the wicker chaise lounges, and dusted my royal blue Honda Fit car. I knew there was no point in cleaning up. At least, right now.

The following afternoon, the sun gleamed with a menacing orange glow, spreading that same eerie light over the garden. What had been a clear cobalt sky in the morning turned dark. Stepping into the garage, I smelled smoke. *Again*, I thought, and hurried back inside.

I hate to think this, but on some level, after massive blazes in three of the past four years, we in Sonoma County have grown accustomed to living with fire. Fifty miles north of San Francisco, this beautiful area where I make my home is known for rolling hills dotted with vineyards that produce world-class wines, towering ancient redwoods, charming small and medium-sized towns, the Russian River flowing out to the Pacific, and a spectacular, wild and rocky coast. In recent years, though, we have also grown famous for fires.

Ever since the October 2017 Tubbs Fire roared over the Mayacamas Mountains from the Napa Valley and ravaged whole neighborhoods in my town of Santa Rosa, Sonoma County residents have learned to live in the belly of the climate change beast. We have permanently packed go-bags and N-95 masks handy, a habit, long before the coronavirus forced us to cover our mouths and noses when we go out. We're signed up to receive text and email alerts from the county sheriff, and local police and fire departments, about fires starting, and hopefully getting controlled, along with warnings and orders to evacuate. We're prepared to hear that PG&E, the electric and gas utility, is planning to shut off power, in response to a forecasted strong wind event or Red Flag Warning, that could send a power line down and spark a destructive fire.

We know the first days of the fire fight will be long and frightening, until the full battery of aircraft and firefighting personnel arrive. We reach out through neighborhood and community networks, to learn who's had to evacuate and offer shelter, if we can. We cheer up at the first signs of containment and wait for the percentages to rise. We figure out what trusted local organizations are collecting money, clothes, or even shampoo and soap, for our neighbors who've lost everything they had. Our spirits go up, as fire engines pour into town, with firefighters from throughout the state and country, and even as far away as Israel and Australia. We scratch out messages of gratitude, plastered with sloppily-drawn red hearts, and post them along the busiest roads, hoping first responders will see them when they drive past.

Fire season was once confined to a portion of the year here in California, ramping up during late September and October, the driest months. But the season has stretched out, growing beyond its original borders, as a dangerous mix of conditions can appear at almost any time. High temperatures, low humidity and strong erratic winds combine with the decades-long practice of suppressing fires, while more and more homes are constructed in or near forests, creating the perfect storm for frequent fires. Added to the mix are what climate change has wrought, with less rain and mountain snow, and resulting droughts, leaving plenty of distressed trees and dry fuels that have made fires larger and more deadly and destructive.

So many blazes have been burning in the nine-county San Francisco Bay Area at the same time lately that several have merged, causing Cal Fire to lump individual fires into massive, overarching complexes. Fires are usually named for where they start. The largest and most destructive of the blazes that roared through the City of Santa Rosa in October 2017, the Tubbs Fire, was named after Tubbs Lane, in the charming Napa Valley town of Calistoga. This year, Cal Fire has labelled each complex, in part, by the cause – lightning. There's the CZU Lightning Complex and the SCU Lightning Complex. Ours is the LNU Lightning Complex.

Like many people I know here, I am not a native Californian. In fact, I'm not a native anything. When people ask where I'm from, I say, "Nowhere." Other times, I might answer, "Everywhere." Then I usually explain. "I grew up in a military family," I say.

My journey to California happened in stages. For a

number of years, I had been living in Washington, D.C., where I started college at American University. I loved the city, especially its diversity. But I also yearned to live closer to nature. When my boyfriend, Marshall, said he wanted to move to the Southwest and work on a documentary film, I jumped at the chance. I'd never been to New Mexico before, but that made the plan even more alluring.

After a year in Albuquerque, we decided to move again. This time, we chose San Francisco.

From the moment we arrived, I knew I'd found where I belonged. I fell hard for the city's colorful Victorians; the awe-inspiring views from the tops of the nearly ninety-degree angled streets, of San Francisco Bay, the Golden Gate Bridge and the Pacific Ocean; and even the chilly, but sometimes romantic, fog. I also couldn't believe that so many wondrous places, including Muir Woods, Point Reyes National Seashore, Big Sur, and the Russian River, could be found only a short drive from the city.

The year after Marshall and I moved to San Francisco, Northern California entered what would turn out to be a severe, years-long drought. I wasn't aware then that throughout history, the land that became the State of California had been prone to such dry spells, some even lasting for decades.

When the drought began in 1978, water-saving devices commonplace today didn't exist. In an effort to use less water, we set bricks down in our toilet bowls. More effectively, we flushed less. The slogan we lived by, one that state and local officials promoted, whether we were at home, work, or in a store or restaurant restroom, was, "If it's brown, flush it down. If it's yellow, it's mellow."

We learned to take five-minute showers, not run the water when we washed dishes or brushed our teeth, and re-use water from the washing machine to keep plants alive. Even then, the water restrictions were so severe, it was a struggle to avoid getting a stiff fine for going above our limit.

In the nearly thirty years I have lived in California, we have experienced many periods of drought. Low-flow toilets, faucets and showerheads, along with water-saving dishwashers and washing machines, have replaced the old water-wasters. After moving into our current house, my husband, Richard, and I pulled out the water-loving lawn and replaced it with a drought-tolerant landscape and low-usage drip irrigation. The City of Santa Rosa reimbursed us for the expense.

Unfortunately, in recent years, no matter how much we conserve, or even the amounts of rain and snow that fall, fire danger in California has only gotten worse. Two years ago, we had a rainier than average winter and more late-season snow. Instead of lessening the fire danger, all that extra water simply promoted additional growth, of fuel ready to combust once the dry summer and fall arrived.

Aside from the actions we need to take to lower carbon emissions that are making California and the entire planet warmer, several changes could be made. So far, they haven't been done. One step would be to prohibit more housing construction in the wildland-urban interfaces close to forests. Experts believe that the proliferation of homes in these areas has caused more wildfires, due to human ignitions. Having large populations living in such vulnerable spots also makes fires more deadly, because firefighters have to put out blazes to save structures and lives, that otherwise could be left to burn, reducing the fuels that contribute to making these fires so deadly. But how do you force people to move away from the places they consider home?

I know many people who lost everything in the fires that swept through Sonoma County in 2017. The three largest blazes that ignited in early October killed twenty-three people and destroyed 5,100 structures, including nearly five percent of the county's housing stock. After sweeping across the mountains that separate Santa Rosa from the town of Calistoga, known for its hot springs, wineries, and spas, the Tubbs Fire wiped out million-dollar homes in the hillside neighborhood of Fountaingrove before leaping across six-lane highway 101, to devastate the modest neighborhood of Coffey Park. Even then, the blaze wasn't done. The fire raced further west, incinerating many of the manufactured homes in a large senior park.

I've listened to harrowing stories from friends and acquaintances of their middle-of-the night escapes, as the sky rained down wind-driven flames. As recently as December 2019, I attended an open house, to view and celebrate the beautiful home that one couple spent the previous two years rebuilding, having lost everything in the Tubbs Fire. Two years after the fire, their gorgeous new home sat surrounded by vacant lots, since many of their neighbors chose not to rebuild, deciding instead to move on.

When the fires first raced across the hills separating Napa and Sonoma Counties, my husband and I were away from home, staying in a cabin next to a bucolic horse pasture, miles from major urban areas in Southern Utah. We had passed through Las Vegas less than a week before, one day after the worst mass shooting in American history. Earlier that morning, sitting in the breakfast room of our hotel in Tehachapi, California, we learned of the horror from the large TV screen, hanging on the opposite wall. Passing the site of the massacre, the Mandalay Bay Resort, on our way to Utah, I noticed that the electronic sign out front, which normally would have been promoting an upcoming concert, was pleading for donations of blood.

In Mount Carmel, Utah, we had little access to the Internet and were generally out and about until sometime after dinner, avoiding the TV news. It was a relief to miss the shooting disaster coverage, which by that point had practically become a daily occurrence. Being in that quiet, beautiful area helped us feel that we'd momentarily stepped back in time, when life might have been a bit less randomly violent.

We learned of the Tubbs Fire from the Internet and friends' and neighbors' emails and calls. On the second day following the start of the Tubbs Fire, when Richard and I were still in Utah, a different blaze, the Nuns Fire, began threatening an area not far from our Santa Rosa house. My husband and I had both signed up to receive text messages from the county's emergency management system and this was how we first learned of the latest threat. Moments later, after we were seated in a nondescript Chinese restaurant on the main street of Kanab, Utah, I went on the Internet. In the days since the start of the fires, our local newspaper, *The Press Democrat,* had been the best source of information. So, I navigated to their site.

Sure enough, the Nuns Fire had moved into Trione-Annadel State Park. Annadel Heights, a neighborhood bordering the park, was under a mandatory evacuation order. The boundaries for the evacuation, Park Trail and Summerfield Drives, were close enough to our house to be worrisome, especially given how rapidly the Tubbs Fire had traveled two days before, but far enough away not to instill panic.

Then I read that a second neighborhood had been evacuated. That neighborhood happened to be ours.

Richard had run to the restroom moments before I read the news. We had already ordered several dishes – cashew chicken and black bean shrimp with string beans. My stomach clenched into a tight knot. I could barely breathe. I read the paragraph again, to make sure it said what I thought. The words confirmed my worst fears.

I waited until Richard sat down before telling him what I now knew. The phone in my right hand, I raised the screen and held it in front of his face.

"Oh, no," was all he said, before punching numbers into his phone. A second later, he moved the phone away from his mouth and said, "I'm calling Wayne."

Wayne was our closest neighbor.

I felt numb. Or rather, anxiety had taken over my mind and body to the point that I'd become nothing more than fear. My stomach ached. I knew I wouldn't manage to get down a single bite of the food we'd just ordered. And what would we do, my racing mind asked. We were a thousand miles away from Santa Rosa. If our house was going to go up in flames, we had no way to save anything.

"Wayne's got his car packed and he says he's ready to go. He wanted to know what he could do about our house."

"Did you leave him a key?" I asked.

"No," Richard said, and shook his head.

There was no question but that we would cut our trip short and leave the following morning. Neither of us considered where we would go, if our house burned or even if the evacuation order remained in effect when we got back to town. Being there, rather than miles away, seemed like what we needed to do. And sleep that night was impossible, of course.

The next morning, we packed the car, just as the sky started to grow light. Wispy clouds were drenched a deep rose. The roosters that freely wandered the property took turns crowing. One dark brown horse and a white one munched grass in the pasture on the other side of the gravel road that led to where we were parked.

As I carried bags of food out to the car, a sense of peace washed over me for the first time since reading the news the night before. The varicolored dawn sky, the leaves on the trees bordering the pasture that were just beginning to turn orange, and the quietly munching horses told me that life would go on, no matter what.

That sense of calm stayed with me, as we drove through the eastern gate into Zion National Park and wound our way past the massive and majestic rock for which the park is known. The early morning light spilling across the rock faces made the landscape glow, adding to the feelings I'd experienced earlier outside the cabin that the most important parts of life would always endure.

An hour later, we stopped for breakfast in the town of St. George. As we waited to order, Richard called our neighbor.

"Oh, that's great," I heard Richard say a moment later.

I did a search for *The Press Democrat* on my phone, feeling a bit relieved from what I'd overheard of Richard's phone conversation. I moved down the most recent series of updates on the fire, finally settling on the paragraph I'd read the night before. Something appeared to be missing, though. I read the paragraph a second time and then checked the updates before and after that one. There was no longer any mention of our neighborhood being under a mandatory evacuation order. (The paper would later acknowledge that the notice about our area had been a mistake.)

"Wayne's unpacked," Richard said. "Everything's fine."

I decided it was time to ask what I hadn't dared ask before.

"If you had time to gather things up, what would you take from the house?"

"I'd grab the documents from the safe," Richard said.

Even though he hadn't asked, I took a moment to consider what I would grab.

"I don't know what I'd take," I said.

# SQUEEZED IN BY DESPAIR

## MEG TUITE

The sky absorbs itself into tiny clusters of strangely beaked branches cutting incisions through the veined hiss of tired blue. Step on to the cackle of leaves beneath your shoes. Wallow your way in and out of trees, skeletal tall, old as aches, and smell darkness bleed into each pore. No sense in pretending what the forest hides. Bodies compost history, groan and gnash dust into rich, brazen dirt damp with the guts of wanderers. A multitude of eyes size up the stench of your leeched family tragedies. The caverns of sad, lonely trails deepen across your face. It's okay. You'll never find yourself alone. A pack of swaying columns covered with bark imperceptibly surround you.

# THERE ARE NO READERS
# OF SILENCE

## MAGDA PHILI

There can be no likes, nor hearts for silence. No clapping of hands. No celebrations. There can be no readers of silence. Just a subdued whisper from the depths of your unshared self in plain dark view mode.

As you scroll down, the whispering voice is asking you not to break the silence. The whispering voice repeats itself each time, with each scrolling, and with each discovery of could-be-friends, could-have-been-friends, cannot-be-friends, will-not-be-friends, once-were-friends juxtaposed side by side like playing cards. As if friendship was a game…

# YOU ARE NOT LISTENING

## LUKE ROLFES

Camila is riding her hoverboard in the cul-de-sac. She has beautiful, long hair and olive skin. She and Matthew are in the same grade, but she has three older sisters, so she knows more about the world than he does.

"Don't freaking touch me, Matty," she says. "Six feet."

"I wouldn't," says Matthew.

The two ride in figure eights through the cul-de-sac--- Camila on her hoverboard and Matthew on his scooter. Their wheels drone on concrete as they fall into a pattern, matching each other's speed. One on the loop, one on the criss-cross.

After a while, Camila says, "Yesterday, I saw a snapping turtle by the bike trail."

"Was it alive?"

"Of course it was alive. Did you know they bite and never let go? It happened to my uncle once. The turtle was stuck to his arm for hours. My dad had to cut the turtle's head off with a saw."

"Like a chainsaw?"

"Just a saw-saw. He had to do it. Nothing else could be done."

"Did your dad bury the turtle?"

"I don't think so."

"What did he do with its body?"

"Threw it in the woods, probably. Maybe just put it in a garbage can."

"What about its head?"

"Jesus, Matty. That's a stupid question if I've ever heard one."

Camila breaks the looping pattern and rolls in a straight line, away from her driveway where sits on cinderblocks her dad's Thunderbird restoration project. Matthew follows her down the hill, past the blue and red playground equipment and the community fishing pond surrounded by shattercane and cattails. There are no other kids outside. The houses are silent, the grass still that awful shade of light yellow. The March air feels like it is trying for rain.

"Hey, there's Dean and Gene," says Matthew. "They live right behind me."

Next to the trail entrance, two older men sit on a park bench. They are holding hands and staring off into the distance of the afternoon. Matthew's parents say he needs to be extra careful around those two. Gene had cancer once. He almost died, but then he got better. Dean, though he doesn't have cancer, has something else. Matthew can't remember what it is.

"You kids look like you are on a mission," says Gene,

the older man on the left.

"Snapping turtles, I guess," says Matthew.

The man on the right, Dean, smiles. He never says much. Gene says, "A dangerous foe. Perhaps you'll need a long net."

Camila and Matthew snoop around the bike trail entrance. They check the tall grass and edge of the stream, but there are no turtles. Still not technically spring, most of the wildlife is in hiding. A few nightcrawlers squirm after Camila rolls over a log. A handful of early water bugs dot the cold water. Neither kid ventures deeply into the surrounding forest. When Matthew looks into the trees, he thinks about a turtle shell half-buried in dirt and weeds--- arms, legs, and tail accounted for but neck ending in nothingness. He doesn't know why, but he shivers.

"Any luck?" Gene asks after a while.

"None," says Matthew.

"You kids staying safe?"

Matthew nods and says "Yes, sir," but Camila doesn't say anything. The two mount their scooter and hoverboard and begin the trek up the hill. The old men on the park bench wave to them as they leave. Matthew waves back.

Camila yells down, "You're the ones who should worry about staying safe, boomer."

As they ride back up the neighborhood hill, Matthew stares as her. At the top, he says, "I don't know why you said that."

She shrugs and says, "I say that stuff to everybody."

And then she cuts in front of him on her hover board.

Her long hair is an auburn waterfall cascading down her back, her clear laugh like a bell. Above his friend, Matthew notices that the houses in the neighborhood all have gray or charcoal colored roofs. And the clouds above them are also gray.

# LETTER-BURNING

## ASHLEY HAJIMIRSADEGHI

That day had been beautiful; it was serene, typical May weather in Maryland. A little muggy, but not muggy enough to chase away the fireflies at dusk. My backyard was full of them, their lights scattered in the darkness, creating mismatched constellations. The first man I ever dated sent a subpar apology letter after the breakup, but that day, upon receiving it, I set it on fire with a lighter. I watched how the inspirational quote he'd written, a cheesy one about finding happiness, curled in on itself and splintered. His name had been the first to go--the flames devoured it whole. *Beauty withers here*, I thought to myself as the breeze picked up, causing the ashes to scatter.

I sat in the middle, where the grass was brittle and withered, cross-legged with that burning letter held out in front of me. It, too, became a star in that stream of firefly lights, a steady one, adding to the tapestry of the night's sky. All living things must die, I realized that. Constellations are dead stars, paper is made of dead trees, a firefly's light dies and sputters back to life. Nothing truly lasts forever.

When there were no more words left to burn, nothing

else left to say or eat, the flame slowly died, disappearing into the void. I danced with the remaining ashes, took a handful and blew them upwards and towards Virgo. And then I had nothing left. The letter was gone. The fireflies withdrew to retire for the night. Alone, I cried, grabbing fistfuls of dying grass and crumbly dirt. How lonely the moon must be, to be the gatekeeper of loss--I mourned for it.

# SNEEZE, INTERRUPTED

## EMILY UDUWANA

I wrinkle my nose
in just the right way
but a noise startles me

and the sneeze
escapes silently,
without relief

it whispers around my nostrils,
leaving me itchy
and unsatisfied,

and it's a good thing, I know,
to suppress a sneeze
during a global pandemic

but the *almost* of it all
reminds me
of those few seconds I spent

so close to you:
breathing the same air,
with fingertips just brushing,

like Adam reaching
out to God,
only to be left with six feet

of space and a sense
of bitter
unfulfillment.

# FLATTENING THE CURVE

## CHRISTINA KAPP

Melinda started driving about the same time everyone else decided to take up walking. It seemed the ideal circumstance. With the pandemic, crowded roads became clear. Traffic dried up like moisture after a rain. People stayed and home and raged at the universe rather than going out and raging at the roads.

The first day she drifted tentatively a few blocks to the empty commuter train station parking lot, her fingers clenched around the wheel at ten and two. She lurched in hard right angles around the vacant lines, learning the weight of this new machine she inhabited, testing her strength against its gasoline-fueled arrogance, its lack of self-awareness, its ignorance. When she drove back to her mother's townhouse, she got out of the car and walked in circles around the driveway, shaking out her arms and stretching her legs in an effort to reclaim her body.

The next day she followed the main road through town and kept going through the next town before she turned around in a Target parking lot and headed home, following the same straight line. With each brake and acceleration, she felt stronger, flexing her driving muscles. As she slipped under stoplights and leaned into corners, she fantasized that she was a warrior training for battle, honing her skills, preparing for some unseen enemy yet to reveal itself.

None of this was true, of course, other than the unseen enemy virus. That was already on the news every day, all anyone could talk about. "Don't forget a mask," her mother said as she handed her daughter the keys. But Melinda had no interest in getting out of the car. She just wanted to drive.

Melinda's mother was worried. "Be careful. Don't go far."

Although Melinda had never really driven a car, she did have a license. In high school everyone took drivers ed. She had sat through the old films of a dad in ill-fitting khakis showing his young son how to test the brake lights and turn signals like everyone else.

She'd even wrestled through her driving lessons and managed to pass the driver's test with a tense "it will do" from the tester. After that, however, Melinda resumed her place in the passenger seat, relieved to have the whole ordeal over with.

After college, Melinda moved to the city. She got a job as an admirative assistant for a company that sold industrial carpet. She met a man who ushered her in and out of Ubers and took her to his glass-walled high-rise apartment that looked out over the river, where she watched the lights of the city twinkling below. People told her she was successful, and Melinda was satisfied with the upward trajectory of her life.

Then the virus came. People stopped riding in elevators and working in cubicles. Ubers stopped coming on demand. The city was frightened, and the man who lived in the high-rise packed a gym bag full of t-shirts and went away. "I'm going to the woods," he said. "All I need is wifi." Melinda was furloughed. No one wanted to buy industrial carpet for vacant offices. She went back to her little apartment and made chamomile tea to soothe her spirits and clear her tear-clogged nose. She sat in her front window and stared at the grey pavement below, watching people drift by like leaves in a stagnant pond.

When she was laid off, Melinda moved back to her mother's townhouse. They sat at the kitchen table and analyzed the virus data on Worldometer, switching between linear and logarithmic graphs, reading articles about staying home to flatten the curve. They did what they were told. They ordered groceries from Amazon. They wore masks. They took their temperatures. They stayed inside, other than their daily walks. Her mother sat at a computer full of checkerboard faces, working. Melinda's body ached with thoughts of her man from the city. She wondered if he was happy.

"Where do you go?" Her mother asked when Melinda had been disappearing with the car every day for two weeks.

"Does it matter?" Melinda said.

On the interstate, Melinda could almost forget about woods and wifi. She fell in love with the long strip of asphalt that felt like a vein of adrenaline running through her, the flash of lane markers a fluttering of eyelashes. Gaining confidence on the largely empty highways, she turned the music up loud on her phone. Queen, Springsteen, Tom Petty. Driving music. At sixty miles an hour with the Rolling Stones her ears, she could rejoin the man from the city if she wanted. She could imagine walking the city streets and wandering through museums if she wanted. But she could also reunite with her high school crush, four-wheel across a mesa in New Mexico with a double agent she'd seen on TV, and drag race with her estranged father down a desert highway. While driving, she was happy, but she was a good daughter, too. She was always home in time for dinner.

As the days passed and her range and speed grew, these

imaginary romances grew as cold as the take out French fries that littered the floor of the car. The music got old as the men who performed it. She came to prefer silence, and one after another she imagined leaving these gaping and shocked men on the side of the road, their shirttails untucked, their three-day beards a blur in her rearview mirror. Alone she sped through the canyons of highway trees, carving though the land like a ship set out to sea. Passenger seat vacant, she put the windows down and let her hair unfurl like a flag in the wind, feeling almost like she could fly.

At night, she and her mother sat on the cat-clawed couch with their phones. They Googled maps of viral spread and read the stories of the sick, the deceased. In tiny handwriting, her mother recorded the number of deaths in the corner of her desk calendar. Melinda scanned her body for symptoms. She felt her chest tighten, her stomach turn.

"The virus is everywhere, Melinda. We have to be careful."

Melinda's stomach ached for her mother.

"It's safe in the car," Melinda said. "Come driving with me."

Her mother said no, she had to work. She had bills to pay and it wasn't so bad—she knew the names of everyone's pets. Bandit, Harley, Cookie Dough, Rosie. She told Melinda to stay home and look for a new job, send out resumes. Melinda nodded—yes, yes, yes—but every morning she filled the car with gas again.

Eventually Melinda drove too fast, too far. A nausea came and went, moving from behind her ears, to the roof her mouth, to the back of her throat. At eighty, ninety miles an hour, she pushed on, willing herself to reach out, hold hands with happier fantasies. Darkness dropped over her like a bowl. She turned on the headlights and kept going. She imagined herself sick, dying. Her eyes burned like dry stones in their sockets and the headlights scrubbed the stories in her mind to skeletons, faces full of teeth and bone. Her eyes closed, her head rocked forward, and she lurched awake to an image of her mother sobbing on the side of the road, her hair blowing in her face, a fistful of plastic flowers in her hand.

It was the first time Melinda felt afraid.

When she saw a blue LODGING sign, she pulled off the highway. Over the tops of the trees a sign glowed like an alien moon in the darkness. She drove toward it.

The sign led her to an empty parking lot surrounding a dark box of a building that reflected her headlights back at her like two glowing eyes. Melinda pulled into the driveway by the entrance and turned off the engine. Her stomach rolled and rumbled like a distant storm.

She reclined her seat, letting her head slip below the waterline of the windows. What were the symptoms of a pandemic? Restlessness, suffocation, anemophobia. Fear of air. What were the symptoms of apocalypse? Burning, drowning, starvation. Disease. There were some things you didn't heal from. She closed her eyes.

Melinda dreamed of being on a glass roof on top of the hotel, looking down through floor after floor of empty, unmade beds, clothes and towels scattered like the aftermath of a rapture. Below, a tow truck made a slow arc across the parking lot, its yellow flasher punching a warning into the wall of night. Melinda watched as her mother, masked in a black bandana, attached her car's front end to the rigging. The car doors flapped open like a metal penguin shedding shoes and travel-sized hand sanitizers and empty soda cups. Her unworn blue masks fluttered into the dark like little birds. She called stop! stop! stop! but her mother never looked up. Her mother got in the passenger side of the tow truck and Melinda could see a man in the driver's seat as they drove away, the yellow flashers like marbles into the night. In the distance, she thought she saw the city, but it was like a glimpse of glitter on skin. There for a moment, then gone again.

Melinda woke covered in sweat. The sun beat down on the car and she struggled to breathe. For a moment she didn't know where she was. She pulled her sleeve down over her hand and wiped a circle in the condensation on the window. The parking lot lay out before her, the asphalt sponging up the sun.

She put the windows down and started the car, cutting across the puzzle of empty spaces painted on the parking lot. It was a new day, and while she thought of her mother hunched over the glowing screen of her phone, she put her foot on the gas and headed for the highway. Her hand reached out into the cool air rushing by the car almost as if she was going to wave goodbye, letting it roll with the waves of her accelerating speed.

# LISTEN TO THE KNOWING

## RALPH MONDAY

Listen to the thin light lancing from a
moon swimming whale-like in cloudy
sea—not the mechanicals beyond the trees,
nor banshee siren, or trucks' elephant rumbles.

Hear instead the hourglass hiss streaming through
veins' theater, heart measuring kettle drum time
here on this deck overlooking mountains raised
eons past, as we, poor infants carry the race's
burdens like weeds, strangers dancing in the
blood.

The snow, the great heron knowing more than Socrates,
time yet unexhausted, listen to all the vanished
family from sea to sea, desert, island, varnished
land. They, too, are there somewhere waiting for the
knowing.

This is the suffering love—not in private, never public—
individual
intimacy passed down like a heirloom heard only in
dark spaces, evaporation of time reforming like dew,
missing words never spoken like soft signs of satisfied
lovers.

Listen to the continents slow movement, drift & hiss of all
the knowing life rooted in the turn of rock, the magnetic,
divine land & hear the false mechanicals drift on & away.

# HOW TO MAKE A CUP
# OF TEA

## RACHEL B. MOORE

Here is how you make a cup of tea. First, clean the kitchen. Sweep the week's crumbs into the sink. Wipe the splattered food from the stove top and backsplash. The compost reeks of rotting citrus. When was the last time you had an orange or squeezed a lemon? Take the compost bucket, and the trash, downstairs.

Spend most of the day standing in the middle of the grimy kitchen doing things that do not need doing. Reorganize the spice rack. Dust the stack of bowls on top of the fridge that no one will ever check for dust, or even notice. Flip through outdated cookbooks with faded photos of gelatined desserts on cake stands, pieces of pale, cubed fruit cocktail and red maraschino cherries suspended through the bright orange Jell-O. You wish you had the wherewithal to turn out something so ridiculously majestic but you can barely manage the effort to rummage in the cabinet to find a pack of cookies.

Fill the kettle with fresh, cold water. Put it on the burner but don't boil it yet.

Set the table with a clean tablecloth. The trick is to make it look like you've done nothing. As though you always have a nicely set table, a clean home. Take the teapot down from the shelf. The big one, the one that can easily serve three or four people, even though it will just be the two of you. There's a few months' worth of kitchen grease on the lid. Wash the teapot in hot water. Leave it to dry beside the stove.

Choose the right kind of tea. If you were alone, like you usually are, you'd go for a smoky earl grey or Russian caravan. Something as strong as the Islay whisky you tell yourself you really should ration. Settle on loose leaf English Breakfast. Innocuous but hearty. It will be better than what your guest is used to. It will make you seem thoughtful.

Spoon some sugar into a small porcelain bowl. Pour some full fat milk into the delicate creamer brought back from your last vacation. Put it back in the fridge to stay cold.

Check the clock. He told you he'd be over by now, but maybe he's just late. Maybe you forgot to change your clock last week. Or maybe he forgot to change his. That whisky is starting to sound better than the tea, but you push that thought out of your mind. Outside, your neighbor is sweeping the landing. It's a comforting sound. Swish, swish.

Grab two mugs from the cabinet. Midnight blue, handmade, the name of the potter scratched into the bottom of each. They are big, café style mugs. You could drown in them. They're good for when he comes around. You think you're so sneaky, refilling his mug when he looks away, telling him he can't leave until he's finished his tea. Stretching a half hour into an hour and a half. But he knows. He has to. Still. You'll take what you can get. You picture his hands wrapped around his mug. His perfectly manicured nails – better than yours. The lopsided wry smile. The way he catches your eyes and holds them, when you usually cannot bear prolonged eye contact from anyone.

Outside, the light has shifted. It is officially late. Turn on the stove to boil the water. Spoon two heaping tablespoons of tea into the teapot. While you wait for the water to boil, even though you don't think you need to bother with it, change your cotton underwear for ones with some lace. Everyday bra for the green one he once told you he liked. Feel ridiculous that you're even making the effort. Put on the gold hoop earrings from your sister. A quick spray of perfume.

The water will boil, the screech of the whistle almost too shrill to bear. Run back into the kitchen to turn it off. Lift the kettle from the burner and fill the teapot. Be careful not to fill it too much or it will overflow and you'll flood the countertop. Put the fancy tea cozy on top of the teapot. It's made of scratchy plaid wool and is thick enough to keep the tea hot for several hours. The apartment will be too quiet. Put on some music. It doesn't matter what. He won't know it anyway. The shadows are starting to climb the walls. Turn on the lights.

You can stand in the kitchen, or sit on the couch, or even sit in the chair by the window and stare out into the street, but it won't make a difference. Like the old adage that a watched pot never boils, a watched street will rarely yield the visitor you long for.

Admit defeat.

In the kitchen, arrange seven cookies on a plate.

Lean up against the counter and eat a couple of cookies straight from the box.

They will be stale. Eat another one.

When the doorbell rings, don't rush to answer it. Finish chewing your cookie. Check your hair in the hallway mirror. When you buzz him in, wait in the doorway for him to climb the stairs.

# VICTORY PARADE

## MICHELLE DROZDICK

It was too hard to keep fighting,

So they went out and celebrated,

Shouting angrily at the corpses,

For trying to belittle their victory.

Before long they stepped over the bodies,

Ignoring the war that had never ended,

Celebrating the wonderful job they'd done,

Bowing to the silent applause of the dead.

# MICHELANGELO'S PALETTE AT EASTER MASS

## ALISE VERSELLA

I could paint a watercolor out of my tears

Salt like vinegar used to dye hard-boiled eggs

Mascara black mixed with shadow cloud, and the glittering mess of blush

The lipstick tip I scraped with my tooth could convert the lapsed Catholic devout

I could make this pandemic art

The way I paint a white light against the contrasting dark

Make dimensions resurrect like Eden was never lost

From my rib and claw comes new dawn

I see a cardinal red like the stained lips of Persephone

She stepped forth from the underworld a queen

The tulips are opening and the bees

Are taking back the reins

Where is your faith?

Redemption can be found in these layers of paint

It is the one thing everlasting a human hand can create

God took the stars and sculpted from their dust

A masterpiece violent and ornate

And when we doubted ourselves he sent us

A child

And isn't that what you see in the eyes of your babes

Some holy light to remind you

Your tears are the flood to wash the land brand-new

I crack open the egg and salt the flesh, remind myself the palette I possess

# SEPTEMBER MOON'S EYE VIEW

## MAUREEN MANCINI AMATURO

They think these marks are craters. They are eyes. To catch me wink or blink or squint, they have to watch patiently. But they don't. I watch them, though, with an ever-changing point of view. On the dark side, I can only imagine what I'm missing.

As the solo body, the only satellite, the mysterious puller of tides and moods, that blue-and-green planet in my watch for time immortal has me guessing right now. I, Lady Moon, am predictable. I have my phases, and I offer them routinely. Lovers, sailors, farmers, everyone knows my course. But since the Earth finished its last turn around our golden ruler, things have changed. That third rock from the sun seems dulled. The beings are hiding. The vibe, well, the vibe is not there.

What are they up to down there? I'm four-billion-plus years old, and I can assure you I've seen it all. Something is going on down there, and it certainly stops me in my orbit. I. haven't a clue what is happening below. Earthlings can be downright foolish, I'd say. I've seen the earth go dark.

I've seen the earth freeze and warm and freeze again. Oh my stars, I've even seen the Earth nearly destroyed, but that was such a very long time ago. Only a few phases back, it seemed that the Earth was trying to speed up. Why just one sun lap prior, the earth was spouting energy and signals from every part of its surface. But I am so confused right now. Where is the motion? Where are those scattered-around-the-planet beings who look up at me when I look down on them? It seems slower down there. There are fewer walking the continents. But they must be there. The electric waves, the sonar, the wireless energy, the invisible signs of life are there. But where is the life? I can't see the people, but I can see their prayer beams. Actually, the prayer beams are blinding lately. So many more than usual.

Perhaps I can do something to bring the beings out of hiding. But what? Reverse my phases? Remain in one phase only for the remainder of this lap around the sun? Maybe I should give it more time, and if nothing changes, if life does not resurface on the blue planet, I'll do something special. No, I'll wait for October 31, when they seem to pay more attention to me. Frankly, I do look stunning in the store windows and on magazine covers and tee-shirts that feature me for the month, if I do say so myself. I do make quite a backdrop for that black silhouette of the woman in the pointed hat riding through the sky. I make quite a backdrop for everything, really. That's why lovers love me.

Back to the issue at hand. Something is keeping those little folks out of view. So many fewer are looking back at me. Been going on for…let's see…almost seven full phases now. There are a few more Earthlings out and about during this last quarter-phase, but not nearly the chaos that used to be. I do hear more bangs. More pops. I see more flashes of light. Tsk, tsk…I hope no one is hurt. It's lonely without those Earth people to entertain. Are they entertaining themselves? Are they falling in love on their own, without me?

Judging by the position of my sister moons out here, I can tell it is time for me to turn in. Just as well, I'm not feeling myself. Perhaps I've caught something from one of those horrid gas emissions. My corona is weak. They, those Earthlings, have no idea what's it's like dealing with a corona.

# CAN YOU HEAR ME?

## NICOLE BLOOMFIELD

"Can you hear me?" I said.

My muffled voice

Flying,

Pleading,

But stopped

By the bordered frame of pixels.

A digitalized dam

Shutting the wave of emotions

From reaching the other side.


"Speak up, please," they said.

I repeat the phrase, "Can you hear me?"

But as my mouth dripped words,

Even I tuned out

Sinking in my thoughts

That is clogged from use--

Because no one wants a flood.

As time ticked in the corner on Zoom,

I still want to reach the other side,

But they said, "We'll try this again another time."

# QUARANTINE

## HOLLY DUNLAP

I am apart from adulthood, devouring
my meals off different plates, one for each
hand, no shoes, no forks needed.

Puzzles move in slow motion. Legos click with
ukulele songs. I don't want to hear this well,

staring at various walls.  Oh, quarantine,
you gape-mouthed spoon, you
rabbit in the grass.

Which mask goes with which mask?

Ignore me, you single-liner.

Put on anything, or nothing.

I don't want to see you;

      I'm afraid we are kin.


We are at best children, and none of us live

to see the results of all our failures.

# LIFE AS WE KNEW IT

## JAMES HANNA

My wife, Mary, and I sit in the living room of our Florida retirement home. We are watching the six p.m. news. The Washington DC police are herding demonstrators from Lafayette Park. The shouts of demonstrators are punctuated by the pop of flash grenades, and lingering drifts of pepper spray obscure them as they retreat. Minutes later, we see the White House occupant standing in front of a church. He is clutching a Bible as though it were a shield.

"That is absolutely surreal," Mary says, but I am not impressed.

"A kleptocrat hiding behind a Bible?" I say. "What's unusual about that?"

"He's so damn artless about it."

I shrug. "His supporters won't care," I say. "They knew he was a rube when they elected him president."

Mary is knitting a sweater, and she pauses to complete a stitch. "Well," she says, "at least karma is catching up to him now."

"Why did karma have to wait for a pandemic?" I say. "Couldn't it have come around sooner?"

Mary goes on with her knitting. "Better late than never."

I turn down the sound on the television. "If karma can't sting with precision," I say, "I think *never* is better than late. Why does it have to kill thousands just to punish one boor?"

Mary, ever sensible, does not look up from her knitting. She says, "Karma will catch up with the protesters too. They're taking the pandemic home with them."

I switch channels but get only more news. Protesters are swarming a highway. "I don't think *all* lives matter to them."

Mary puts down her knitting. "Watch your mouth," she cautions. "Do you want to be known as a racist?"

"I don't want to be known at all," I say, then I recite from "The Second Coming." "'Things fall apart,'" I parrot. "'The center cannot hold.'"

"Again with that damn poem?" Mary mutters.

"What do you have against Yeats?"

"Nothing," says Mary. "But he is kind of stale. That poem's getting beaten to death these days."

I am comfortable with the familiar, so I recite another line. "'The best lack all conviction while the worst are full of passionate intensity.'"

"That poem gives you too much credit," says Mary.

"What do you mean by that?"

"Well, you've *never* been very passionate."

"At least, I'm not spreading disease."

"Maybe not," she says, "but you *are* spreading boredom. A little passion on your part would be welcome now and then."

"Do I have to burn police cars?" I joke.

"That's not what I meant," says Mary.

132

"We're housebound," I say. "We can't *take* a vacation. Life as we know it is over."

"I *know* we're housebound," says Mary. "But for *you*, that's a bit too convenient. Do you really think you can sit there all day and make no effort at all?"

"Do you actually expect me to recover the past?"

"No, but I expect you to try."

"Well, what do you want me to do?"

"Figure it out," she replies.

~ ~ ~

Determined to resurrect life as we knew it, I go on the internet. Our days of carefree trips are done, our days of dining out are done, but I hope to at least find some semblance of a romantic getaway. As if by divine coincidence, a colorful ad pops up. It features a restaurant with a porch light so green that it might have beckoned Jay Gatsby, and a voice you could pour over waffles is making a soothing pitch. *"An intimate dinner for two? No problem. Wines from the south of France? No problem. Candlelight while you dine? No problem. The Auld Lang Syne Bistro has it all, and we even supply the candles. Just combine any items on our menu for a sumptuous three-course dinner. In less than half an hour, your meal will be ready for curbside pickup."*

I slowly scroll down the menu and am impressed by what I see. The menu features pork schnitzel, stuffed salmon, and duck breast with apricot chutney. It lists honey-baked chicken, prime rib with fresh herb sauce, and burgundy beef stew. It has garden and strawberry salads and fifteen types of soup, and for dessert, it offers a choice between butter tarts and chocolate mousse. On top of this, the menu suggests a wine for every course. It lists forty types of wine, all from the south of France, and a lively description and food pairing accompanies every wine. For example, Babar Bordeaux is described as a wine with a whisper of boldness—a wine that goes well with schnitzel and very rare prime rib.

I summon Mary to my computer and ask her to check out the ad. "This could bring back life as we knew it," I say.

Mary sits down and scrolls through the ad. "We never knew life this good."

"Shall we pick out a couple of dinners and dine by candlelight?"

"I'm allergic to fish," says Mary, "and ducks are too cute to eat. But I wouldn't mind having a prime rib dinner with maybe a garden salad."

"What kind of dressing?"

"Vinaigrette."

"And for dessert?"

"Surprise me."

"What about wine?"

"Whoa there, stud. You know I never drink wine."

I write down Mary's order and include a butter tart, then I carefully study the menu and decide what to get for myself. When I have made some adventurous choices, I feel like a connoisseur, and I read my selections to Mary as though reciting an epic poem. "Vichyssoise with Chardonnay, burgundy stew with Merlot, chocolate mousse with plum wine—that oughta make a change."

"What kind of change are you talking about? Are you trying to turn into a lush?"

"I'm trying to do something romantic," I say.

"Well, I don't want a romantic drunk."

I explain to Mary that the bottles are small, but she only rolls her eyes.

~ ~ ~

I go online to place our orders and am stymied by all the instructions. It seems getting back life as we knew it will not be a simple task. First, I have to secure the location of an Auld Lang Syne Bistro near us—apparently, this intimate restaurant is part of a national chain. After securing a local location, I must confirm a pick-up time then I have to list the color and model of the car I intend to bring. I am forced to slog through forty more questions before moving on to the menu—questions so stark and invasive that I should have probably been read my rights. *Did you sneeze today? Did you masturbate? Did you wash your hands after peeing?* Since a single irreverent answer would probably blacklist me, I answer each of these questions with a watchmaker's care.

By the time I arrive at the menu, my frustration has only begun. Each food item I order lists dozens of subcategories. For example, my request for burgundy stew unleashes this torrent of queries: *Do you have any food allergies? Would you like grain or grass-fed beef? Would you like gluten-free gravy?* The questions go on and on like a nonstop merry-go-round.

By the time I have chosen the food items, I feel like I've battled a hydra, but when I come to the wine list, my frustration hits a new peak. I must pick from a dozen different brands for every wine I choose; I must also list the year of the wine and the region in France I prefer. *Sorry, not available* pops up so frequently that I make alternate selections as desperately as I might have played Russian roulette. "Mary was right," I mutter. "I should have left out the wines."

It takes me almost four hours to get the order completed. The bill comes to three hundred dollars. I enter my credit card number. I feel like I've passed the bar exam when my order is confirmed.

~ ~ ~

I drive to the Auld Lang Syne Bistro to make my curbside pickup. It is located in a shopping center twenty minutes from our house. The restaurant, which looks like a Tudor home, has an expansive parking lot, and a dozen cars sit in front of the place in numerically marked parking spaces.

I pull into one of the parking spaces and read the instructions on the placard. The message says, *Phone us when you arrive and announce your parking space number. Somebody will be out with your order.* I punch-dial the phone number on the placard. I only receive a recording. I leave a message and wait, but I do not get a response.

After half an hour, I spot someone rushing from car to car. She is a short, wiry woman wearing a cloth mask that makes her look like a bandit. When she reaches my car, she taps on the driver's window. She steps back as I lower the glass.

"Hon," she says, "this ain't my fault. I only hand out the meals."

"What's not your fault?" I ask stonily.

"The chef didn't show up for work."

"That's not my fault either," I say.

The woman wags her head—she seems put off by my comment. "His wife ran off with her hairdresser, hon. She left him a Dear John note. Ya expect a fella to show up for work after going through something like *that*?"

I listen without sympathy. This is too much information. "Will he be back tomorrow?" I say.

The woman shuffles her feet. "If he doesn't kill the slut—yeah," she snaps. "That's no way to treat your husband. But try us again tomorrow, hon—just submit another order. And ask for me—my name is Jan. I'll make sure ya get real quick service."

"Thank you, Jan," I say.

She dashes to another car.

I decide to drop by McDonald's as I pull out of the parking lot.

~ ~ ~

I return home with a couple of Big Macs and tell Mary about my experience. When she looks at me impatiently, my palms begin to sweat. "The chef's wife eloped with her hairdresser." I bleat. "What can I do about that?"

"I'll *tell* you what you can do," says Mary. "Go online, make sure your order is canceled then never go there again."

"So how will we get back life as we knew it?"

"There must be another way."

When I turn on my computer, I have serious reservations. I wonder where our country would be if our founders had given up so easily. Infused with the spirit of Jefferson, I resolve to make a stand. For the first time ever, I decide that I will ignore one of Mary's requests. After performing some wrist stretching exercises to stave off carpal tunnel, I recite the first line of "The Second Coming" as though it's a battle hymn. "'Turning and turning in the widening gyre, the falcon cannot hear the falconer.'"

I make sure my previous order is canceled then I laboriously fill out another, including all the food items I listed earlier today. This time it only takes me three hours because I eliminate the wines. When I spot a box marked *Special Remarks*, I express my condolences to the chef—it seems the roaring pandemic has given me empathy. I decide to grant the poor man time to recover from his heartbreak, so I set my pickup hour for six p.m. the following day.

~ ~ ~

The next evening, I leave the house when Mary isn't looking. I drive to The Auld Lang Syne Bistro and park in one of its numbered spaces. Jan is standing in the parking lot like a sentry guarding a fort. She walks up to my car and taps on the driver's window. I roll the window down.

I think she is smiling behind her mask. "Your order is about ready," she says.

"How's the chef?" I ask.

She drops her gaze. "He ain't in a very good mood, hon. He believes in fine dining—not takeout."

"I'm sorry to disappoint him," I say.

Her voice grows sympathetic, or perhaps the mask softens her tone. "Don't let that bother you, hon—I want you to have a nice evening. Besides, this bug ain't gonna last for more 'an another month."

Apparently Jan is a Trump supporter—who else would believe such crap? I want to expand her thinking, but this is not the time. I don't want to give her a lecture if it might tempt her to spit in my food.

~ ~ ~

Holding a bulging paper sack, I walk through our front door. I carry the sack into the living room where Mary is sipping iced tea.

"Where have you been?" asks Mary. "Oh, don't tell me—I already know. You were out recovering life as we knew it."

"I'm on a mission?" I say.

"Really," says Mary. "It's just a meal."

"So was the Last Supper."

I dump out the sack on the coffee table and flinch when I hear Mary gasp. Its contents consist of two candles and a dozen fish sandwiches.

"You're kidding," says Mary.

"I wish I were."

"Did you look at the receipt?"

"This isn't my fault," I stammer. "All I did was pick up the meals."

"You *didn't* pick up the meals," Mary snaps. "Not unless you ordered fish."

I grit my teeth like a boxer. "Next time I'll get it right."

~ ~ ~

As I open the link to the Auld Lang Syne site, I'm glad that we at least got the candles. This tiny victory sustains me as I fill out a third order. It takes me another three hours to log our original meals, and I console myself by leaving a very modest tip.

Mary watches me as I labor. "Are you really this obsessed?"

"The falcon cannot hear the falconer," I say, and I press the checkout button.

Mary ignores me for the rest of the day, and she makes me sleep on the couch. As I leave our house the following evening, she does not say a word.

I drive back to the Auld Lang Syne Bistro. The parking lot is empty. I should take this as a warning, but I am too focused for that. Instead, I see it as a sign that the service will be fast.

Jan spots me from the restaurant door and strolls out to my car. When I open the driver's window, she hands me a ten-dollar bill.

"Keep it, hon," she snaps. "You must need it more than me."

"You'll get a bigger tip," I say, "when you start getting my orders correct."

When I explain about the fish sandwiches, she chuckles behind her mask. "I guess that means that some rednecks got prime rib and vichyssoise."

"You're taking this very lightly," I say.

"Naw, you're gettin' too worked up. You don't need to get this excited about a coupla lousy meals."

"It's not about prime rib," I say. "It's about getting life back as we knew it."

"Ya can't go home again, hon," she says. "Haven't you read that book."

I look at her incredulously. "You've read Thomas Wolfe?"

She places her hands on her hips and scowls. "I also read Shakespeare, hon. I hope that don't upset you. You look like the sort of fella who likes to keep things in a box."

Again, she has given me more information than I care to assimilate. "Why don't you go box up my order," I say. "Make sure you bring the receipt."

"As you like it," she jokes, and she goes back into the restaurant.

Returning five minutes later, she hands me a full shopping bag. The receipt is stapled to the bag and I comb through every item. "It looks like you got it right," I say.

She dramatically slaps her forehead. "Oh, thank god. I don't wantcha missin' out on life as you knew it."

~ ~ ~

I place the food on our coffee table and open two of the plastic boxes. Both boxes contain duck a l'orange. Mary stares in disbelief.

"That's not even on their menu," I say.

"Did you check your receipt?" Mary says.

"I went over every item. I was sure they had it right."

I hand the receipt to Mary. She does not glance at it. "They must have stapled it to the wrong bag. You should have looked inside the boxes."

"Will you settle for duck a l'orange?" I plead

"You know I don't eat duck."

"Well, if we can't get back life as we know it, we may as well settle for duck."

"You eat it," says Mary. "I'm making myself a peanut butter sandwich."

After Mary vanishes into the kitchen, I guiltily devour my duck. It is utterly delicious, but that does not shake my resolve. I am more determined than ever to get my order right.

~ ~ ~

Mary no longer speaks to me—it's like she has taken a vow of silence. But with destiny in the balance, I can put no stock in that. So every day for the rest of the week, I order two meals from the restaurant, and each day my endeavor is thwarted by some karma run amok. On one occasion, Jan phoned me to say the power went off in the kitchen, so most of the food had spoiled and had to be tossed out. On another occasion, she texted that the chef had been thrown in jail—apparently, he violated a stay-away order and beat the shit out of his wife. On a third occasion, I actually made it as far as the parking lot, but Jan came out of the restaurant and told me that the new chef had just sneezed on my food.

"Why don't you give it up, hon," she said. "Your wife must be fit to be tied. I'm thinking of blowing this pop stand myself and taking an acting class."

"I'll miss you," I said, and I meant it.

"I'll miss you too, hon," she replied.

I gave her a fifty dollar tip, perhaps to placate the Gods, and I drove back home to go online and order two more meals.

Yes, Mary has stopped speaking to me, but what can I do about that? I can hear destiny calling—a summons I dare not defy. So I sit down at my computer, and I go back to that site. I know I will get back life as we knew it. Perhaps on my very next try.

# MIGRANT ENTROPY

## INKLINGFAIR

She dog-paddles through the shallows,

gaping through goggles at ocean-floor creatures,

silver black-striped fish darting beneath, gills fanning out.

When her back starts to burn with drying salt

she flips over, belly to the sky, to the blinding

sun red against her eyelids.

Squinting at the horizon she pretends

there is no shore for miles around.

Beneath, silently waving black spines,

a sea urchin beckons

from a slow-dying reef.


She is, as she ever was, proud and distant,

her blood watered-down honey from the rains, her
memories crumbly

sepia-and-brackish-flood prints. She, the first coal caught
by high tide, driftwood spitting blue

hissing in the dunes.

She walks among the mangroves humming, dress rustling

against her thighs, her eyes evolved from the soft fishlike
dullness of years past, near-reptilian.

People drifted by in boats, by her

camouflaged in the banks' shadows.

She had faded in with the island, with the sea and the sea-
people

her city colors bleached out by the harsh sun

reflected and magnified a thousand times by the clear blue
waters.

She belonged to them now, a ghost.


When she wakes to the riff of metal beasts

leaking petrol and crunching pebbles under

rubber, of wind-up people ticking by

in tight city shoes

she is not alone in the cacophony, she is hemmed in

as attic clothes nestle mothballs

muffling sublimation.

She is nothing but solid air

hurtling toward disorder, her

natural state.

# CONTRIBUTORS

***Maureen Mancini Amaturo***, New York based fashion/beauty writer and columnist with an MFA in Creative Writing, teaches writing, leads the Sound Shore Writers Group, which she founded in 2007, and produces literary events. Her fiction, essays, creative non-fiction, comedy, and articles have appeared in many magazines, journals, and anthologies including: The Dark Sire (Bram Stoker Award and TDS Creative Award nominee), Boned, Every Day Fiction, Coffin Bell Journal, Drunken Pen, Dime Show Review, Flash Non-Fiction Food Anthology (Woodhall Press,) Things That Go Bump (Sez Publishing,) Film Noir Before It Was Cool (Weasel Press), and Points In Case, Little Old Lady Comedy.. A handwriting analyst diagnosed her with an overdeveloped imagination. She's working to live up to that.

***Nicole Bloomfield*** is a writer from Hong Kong who had written for *Young Post* and *Medium* where her articles have been curated and featured in prestigious publications, including one of the top 30 publications on the platform. When she's not dabbling in writing projects, you can find her playing running or reading.

***Sarah Cavar*** is a PhD student, writer, and critically Mad transgender-about-town, and serves as Managing Editor at *Stone of Madness Press*. Author of two chapbooks, A HOLE WALKED IN (*Sword & Kettle Press*) and THE DREAM JOURNALS (*giallo lit*), they have also had work in *Bitch Magazine, Electric Literature, The Offing, Luna Luna Magazine,*

*Superstition Review*, and elsewhere.

**Michelle Drozdick** is a NYC-based writer and performer, with works recommended by the *New York Times, Time Out NY,* and *We Heart Astoria.* She's previously been published in *Points in Case, Maudlin House, Robot Butt,* and elsewhere.

**Holly Dunlap** has been published in *Past Ten*, an anthology called *Feckless Cunt,* and *300 Days of Sun.*

**C. D. Frelinghuysen** is a writer and pediatrician in Oakland. He has prose out or forthcoming from *Puerto del Sol, Gone Lawn, Flapperhouse,* and elsewhere.

**Ashley Hajimirsadeghi**'s work has appeared in Into the *Void Magazine, Corvid Queen,* and *cahoodaloodaling,* among others. She is a poetry reader at *Mud Season Review* and *Ex/Post,* attended the International Writing Program's Summer Institute, and was a Brooklyn Poets Fellow.

**James Hanna** is a retired probation officer and a former fiction editor. His work has appeared in over thirty journals including *Sixfold, The Literary Review,* and *Literally Stories.* His books, three of which have won awards, are available on Amazon.

**AE Hines** AE Hines is a poet who grew up in North Carolina and currently resides in Portland, Oregon. Winner of the 2020 *Red Wheelbarrow* prize, he is a recent *Pushcart* and *Best of the Net* nominee, and was a finalist for the 2020 Sewanee Review Annual Poetry Contest and Montreal International Poetry Prize. His work is widely published in anthologies and literary journals such as *Potomac Review, Tar River Poetry, Atlanta Review, California Quarterly, I-70 Review* and *Hawaii Pacific Review.* His first full-length collection, "*Any Dumb Animal,*" is forthcoming from *Main Street Rag* Publishing in 2022.

***Inklingfair***'s poetry has been published by indie zines *Paper Monster Press* and *The Rising Phoenix Review,* and will appear in the *First Permission Granted* poetry anthology.

***Christina Kapp*** teaches at the Writers Circle Workshops in New Jersey and her work has previously appeared in *Passages North, Hobart, Crack the Spine, The MacGuffin, PANK, Pithead Chapel* and elsewhere. Her fiction has been nominated for Best of the Net awards and a Pushcart Prize. She welcomes you to follow her on Twitter @ChristinaKapp

***Blake Kilgore*** grew up in Tornado Alley, spending most of his first three decades in Texas and Oklahoma. Now, he lives in New Jersey with his wife and four sons, where he's beginning his twenty-third year (virtually) teaching history to junior high students. That's how his love for story began - recounting the (mostly) true stories from olden times. Eventually, he wanted to tell stories of his own, and you can find some of these in *Lunch Ticket, Deep South Magazine, Oracle, Rathalla Review, Crack the Spine,* and other fine journals.

***Tain Leonard-Peck*** is a high school student. He writes plays and novels, paints, and composes music. He's a competitive sailor, skier, and fencer. He currently lives on a family farm on Martha's Vineyard, but he's lived all over the world as well. He can construct his own laminar flow hood, knit his own blankets, and haggle for flowers on five continents. He thinks the world is a place of wonders, and he loves traveling to see more of it. He has lived in caves, dived with sharks, and not been defenestrated by a temperamental donkey named William Shakespeare. He is frequently bitten by geese.

***Laura Celise Lippman***'s work has appeared in *Crosswinds, Mobius: The Journal of Social Change, Poetry on Buses, Pontoon Poetry, Poydras Review, Journal of Family Practice*, and *Vashon Island Ekphrastic Exhibit*. Lippman has attended numerous writing conferences, including the Port Townsend Writer's Conference, Seattle 7 Writers Conferences, and Hugo House Workshops. She attended Bryn Mawr College where she studied with Kate Millett and Lila Karp in one of the nation's first women's studies programs. Lippman studied at the University of Oregon and received her M.D. from the Medical College of Pennsylvania. She practiced medicine for thirty-seven years and raised two children with her husband in the Pacific Northwest. She enjoys the outdoors and shares her love of the natural world with her grandchildren and friends.

***Rosaleen Lynch***, an Irish community worker and writer in the East End of London, pursues stories conversational, literary and performed. Words in *Jellyfish Review, EllipsisZine, Fish, The London Reader, Mslexia* and other lovely places like *Crack the Spine*.

***Deniel Sean Macapal*** is a graduate under the BA Communication Arts program at the University of the Philippines Los Baños. When she isn't slaving away at her nine-to-five, Deniel spends most of her free time remotely working on passion projects for Apokries Productions as its co-founder and lead visual artist. She now lives with her sister and their two dogs in Makati City.

***Ralph Monday*** Ralph Monday is Professor of English at Roane State Community College in Harriman, TN., and has published hundreds of poems in over 100 journals. A chapbook, *All American Girl and Other Poems*, 2014. A book *Empty Houses and American Renditions*, 2015. A Kindle chapbook *Narcissus the Sorcerer*, 2015. A poetry collection, *Bergman's Island & Other Poems* by *Terror House Press*, 2021, and a humanities text was published by Kendall/Hunt in 2018. Vol. 2 of the humanities text is expected in 2021.

***Rachel B. Moore*** earned her MFA in Creative Writing from Lesley University in 2012. Her short story, "Missing", appears in the collection *Debs: Four Women Writers on the Verge*. Rachel's literary obsessions include disappearances of all kinds, missing people, architecture, travel and displacement/disconnection.

After losing three close family members at a very impressionable age, ***Stephen Stratton Moore*** tributes this experience as greatly influencing him as a writer in the way that he looks at things. It gave him a richer appreciation for our connectedness as human beings and stoked an inner passion to revel in the bittersweet nuances of those bonds. Stephen is a published writer, musician, and graphic designer. Since January 2020, Stephen's stories have appeared in *Adelaide Literary Magazine* and *Hedge Apple, The Literary Magazine*.

***W. T. Paterson*** is a two-time Pushcart Prize nominee,

MFA candidate for Fiction at the University of New Hampshire, and graduate of Second City Chicago. His work has appeared in over 80 publications worldwide including *The Forge Literary Magazine, The Delhousie Review,* and *Fresh Ink.* A number of stories have been anthologized by *Lycan Valley, North 2 South Press,* and *Thuggish Itch.* He spends most nights yelling for his cat to "Get down from there!"

**Magda Phili** works as a freelance translator and writes short, flash and micro fiction and non-fiction. She has a short story, written in Italian, published in the *Lingua Madre 2020 Anthology.* She lives in the Emilia Romagna region in Italy.

**Devin Porter** is a New York based playwright, poet, fiction writer, and dramaturg. Devin uses his writing to grant voice to the ones who aren't heard. Born and raised on Long Island, Devin expresses his own individuality and unique style similar to his home state. His works analyze and examine the areas of race, political ideals, social class, and identity. Devin graduated with honor distinctions from the University of Albany with a B.A in English, where he was a three-time Spellman Academic Award winner.

**David E. Poston**'s work has appeared recently or is forthcoming *in The MacGuffin, Pembroke Magazine,* and the *North Carolina Literary Review.* He is the author of three poetry collections, most recently "Slow of Study," and a co-editor of *Kakalak.*

**Bill Pruitt** is a fiction writer, storyteller and poet, and an

Assistant Editor with *Narrative Magazine*. His short stories have appeared in *Crack the Spine Literary Magazine, Midway, Indiana Voice Journal,* and *Hypertext.* Bill has published poems in such places as *Ploughshares, Anderbo.com* and *Cottonwood.* He has two chapbooks with *White Pine* and *FootHills*; and self-published "Walking Home" from the *Eastman House.*

**David Ricchiute** lives in Indiana and in Kentucky. A volunteer at the Northern Indiana Center for Hospice Care and the Beacon Children's Hospital Ronald McDonald House, he is the author of *Uncertain in the Worst Way* (Main Street Rag Publishing, 2020) and *So Everyone Else Will Know* (Aldrich Press, 2018).

**Luke Rolfes** grew up outside of Des Moines, Iowa. His book Flyover Country won the Georgetown Review Press Short Story Collection Contest, and his fiction and essays have appeared in numerous journals including *North American Review, Bat City Review, Connecticut Review, Baltimore Review,* and others. He is a graduate of the MFA program at Minnesota State University and currently teaches creative writing at Northwest Missouri State University, where he serves as co-editor for *The Laurel Review.* He mentors in the AWP Writer to Writer Program.

**Liza Sofia** is a 21 year old university student in Rochester, New York currently studying French and Economics. Her passion for the literary arts started in early childhood, and by age 17, she finished her first book manuscript. Liza has hopes of becoming a novelist.

**Patty Somlo**'s most recent book, "Hairway to Heaven

Stories," was published by *Cherry Castle Publishing*, a small Black-owned press committed to literary activism. "Hairway" was a Finalist in the American Fiction Awards and Best Book Awards. Two of Somlo's previous books, "The First to Disappear" (*Spuyten Duyvil*) and "Even When Trapped Behind Clouds: A Memoir of Quiet Grace" (*WiDo Publishing*), were also Finalists in several book contests. She has published widely in literary journals and anthologies, received Honorable Mention for Fiction in the Women's National Book Association Contest, and had an essay selected as Notable for Best American Essays 2014.

**William R. Stoddart** is a poet and fiction writer who lives in Pennsylvania. His work has appeared or is forthcoming in *The Orchards Poetry Journal, Iris Literary Journal, Main Street Rag, Third Wednesday, The Pedestal Magazine, Adirondack Review and Ruminate Magazine*. His poetry has been nominated for a Pushcart Prize.

**Mishal Imaan Syed** is a student at UCLA studying cognitive science and English literature. Her work has previously been published at *Page and Spine Review, Scarlet Leaf Review*, and the *Los Angeles Times*.

**Rae Theodore** is the author of "My Mother Says Drums Are for Boys: True Stories for Gender Rebels" and "Leaving Normal: Adventures in Gender." Her stories and poems have appeared in numerous publications, including *Our Happy Hours: LGBT Voices from the Gay Bars* and *Sinister Wisdom*. Rae is the winner of the 2020 Joan Ramseyer Memorial Poetry Contest and immediate past president of the Greater Philadelphia Chapter of the Women's National

Book Association. She lives in Royersford, Pennsylvania, with her wife, kids and cats.

*Linda Trice* graduated from Howard University, received a MFA from Columbia University's Writing Division and earned a PhD in Black Studies from the Center for Minority Studies. She taught at Lincoln University, CUNY's Borough of Manhattan Community College, SUNY's Empire State College and was a Fellow at Hambidge, Millay and VCCA. Linda is a member of The Authors Guild. Her short stories have been published in several literary journals including *Rigorous: A Literary Journal by Black, Indigenous and People of Color, Penumbra: Black Lives Matter Edition, Short Stories Bimonthly, Colorlines, Papyrus, Sarasvati, Candlelight Journal, The Naples Review, Ink, Idiolect, Small Pond Magazine,* and others.

*Meg Tuite* is author of four story collections and five chapbooks. She won the Twin Antlers Poetry award for her poetry collection, "Bare Bulbs Swinging". She teaches writing retreats and online classes hosted by Bending Genres. She is also the fiction editor of *Bending Genres* and associate editor at *Narrative Magazine.*

*Emily Uduwana* is a poet and graduate student with recent publications in *Miracle Monocle, Eclectica Magazine,* and the *Owen Wister Review.*

*Alise Versella* is a Pushcart-nominated contributing writer for Rebelle Society whose work has most recently been published in *Steam Ticket* and *Poydras* among various others. Versella performs spoken word throughout New Jersey. Her debut book "When Wolves Become Birds" is now available from *Golden Dragonfly Press*.

***Jami Williams*** is an MFA candidate at Lindenwood University. She teaches English, broadcasting, journalism and publications at Mexico High School in Mexico, Missouri, where she makes her home with her husband and son.

VISIT CRACKTHESPINE.COM FOR MORE
ANTHOLOGIES, OR TO SUBMIT YOUR WORK TO
OUR PUBLICATIONS